Also from Franklin Covey Co.

The 7 Habits of Highly Effective People
Principle-Centered Leadership
First Things First
Daily Reflections for Highly Effective People
First Things First Every Day
The Breakthrough Factor
To Do . . . Doing . . . Done: A Creative Approach to Managing
*   Projects and Effectively Finishing What Matters Most*
The Power Principle
The 10 Laws of Successful Time and Life Management
The 7 Habits of Highly Effective Families
The 7 Habits of Highly Effective Teens
The Nature of Leadership
Living the 7 Habits
Franklin Planner
The 7 Habits of Highly Effective Teens Journal

DAILY
Reflections for Highly Effective Teens

SEAN COVEY

A Fireside Book
Published by
Simon & Schuster

FIRESIDE
Rockefeller Center
1230 Avenue of the Americas
New York, NY 10020

Designed by Stan Drate/Folio Graphics
Illustrated by Raeber Graphics Inc.

Manufactured in the United States of America

10   9   8   7   6   5   4   3   2   1

Library of Congress Cataloging-in-Publication Data is available.

ISBN 0-684-87060-6

Foreword

Hi. My name is Sean and I wrote the book *The 7 Habits of Highly Effective Teens*, which this little book is based on. The purpose of this book is to help you better understand and live the 7 Habits. I must admit, living the 7 Habits ain't no cakewalk. It takes work. The good news is you don't have to be perfect to see results. Just living some of the habits some of the time can make a huge, positive difference in your life. And that's where this book comes in. It breaks down the habits into bite-sized morsels so that you can take one little bite each day. You don't have to swallow the whole thing at once.

Reading just a few words each day is a small thing but will go a long way. In fact, I've become convinced that little things rule the world. Take relationships, for example. In relationships, it's the little things that are the big things. I think we've all experienced how a kind note, a smile, a compliment, an apology, or a hug can completely turn your day around.

I remember taking a literature class from a professor who was considered very controversial because of his stance on some issues. Because I didn't know if he liked me, and because he had a reputation for being a troublemaker, I decided I didn't like him. But that all changed one day. I went to him to ask for an extension on a paper I had not yet finished (I had a good reason for being late) and was surprised by what I learned. He was kind, he was understanding, he cared. And he gave me more time to finish my paper. I walked out of his office wanting to tell the whole world, "Hey, this is a great guy!" That one little act of kindness turned my feelings toward him upside down. Just like that.

And what about the power of little thoughts? How often has one little thought or idea made a big impression on you, for good or bad?

On one occasion I was telling my dad how my fears of failing on the football field were holding me back and he looked me square in the eye and said, "Sean, never let your fears make your decisions for you. You make them." I've never been able to get that little thought out of my head. It haunts me. Whenever I get scared about trying something new or jumping outside my comfort zone, I hear those words ringing, "Never let your fears make your decisions." This little thought has given me the courage, again and again, to act in the face of fear and not look back.

I'm sure you have your own set of little thoughts that have been big in your life.

Little habits can also have huge impact. For example, I have a friend who has the little habit of reading the newspaper every day. As a result, the guy is up-to-date on every current event, every political issue, every debate, every letter to the editor. What a big, positive difference this little habit has made in his life! And I have another friend who has the little habit of sending e-mails to all his pals regularly. It's no wonder he has so many friends.

Doing the little things is also the key to living the 7 Habits. Since you're never going to master the habits overnight, you're better off starting with the little things, or what I call "baby steps." Let me share with you seven baby steps (one for each habit) that all have big payoffs.

HABIT 1—BE PROACTIVE

Stop worrying about things you can't control, like the weather, who your parents are, or how your boyfriend or girlfriend might treat you today. Instead, focus on what you can control, like your attitude, your decisions, and your response to whatever happens to you. This little step is the first big step in gaining control over your moods.

Habit 2—Begin with the End in Mind

Write down your goals. When I speak to teen groups I often ask, How many of you have goals? Most hands go up. I then ask, How many of you have written down your goals? Very few hands go up. One of the primary reasons we fail to reach our goals is because we haven't written them down. Consequently, our goals aren't clear enough or specific enough. Writing them down will help you clarify what it is you really want to accomplish and when you want to accomplish it. Remember, a goal not written is only a wish.

Habit 3—Put First Things First

Take fifteen minutes at the beginning of each week to plan your week. Block out time for your most important events in advance. A little bit of up-front planning each week will go a long way in helping you get more done.

HABIT 4—THINK WIN-WIN

When Ronald Reagan was president, he supposedly had a sign in his office that read, "We will accomplish more if we don't care who gets the credit." How true it is. Get into the habit of sharing recognition and praise whenever you get it. The people you share the recognition with will love you for it. As an added bonus, it will make you feel big inside.

HABIT 5—SEEK FIRST TO UNDERSTAND, THEN TO BE UNDERSTOOD

Learn to use these words, "What do you think?" Often we are so concerned about making sure that everyone knows *what we think* that we never listen to them. The fact is, people love to tell you what they think. But don't just say these words, mean them. The next time you're in a conversation, ask, "So what did you think about the dance last night, Jessica?" "Mom, what do you think I should do?" There's a whole new world out there just waiting to be discovered and the key is in your little ears. Give 'em a try.

HABIT 6—SYNERGIZE

Learn to appreciate differences. The next time you run into someone and feel yourself judging that person because they dress, talk, think, speak, or look different, stop yourself and think about what you do have in common instead. Remember, they might be judging you in the same way you're judging them. There is always a lot more common ground than first meets the eye.

HABIT 7—SHARPEN THE SAW

Take a few minutes each day to renew yourself spiritually. Our world is so fast-paced, so loud, and so full of competing messages that it's easy to let the spiritual side of your life get smothered. Don't let that happen to you. Each day read inspiring literature, take a walk, meditate, listen to uplifting music, pray, or do whatever renews you spiritually. Fill your well each day and it will never run dry. Of all the little baby steps we've talked about, this is probably the most important.

Anyhow, forewords are supposed to be short, so I better wrap this up. Let me just say this: I hope that you'll take a moment each day to reflect upon the little words in this book and that you'll never forget the power of the little things. In reality, they're big suckers. Truly, out of small things, great things are achieved. Happy trails.

Sean

P.S. I want to hear from you. I want to know all about your experience with the 7 Habits. How have they helped you? Please send me your stories, thoughts, and experiences on the 7 Habits via e-mail at *7Hteen@7habits.com* or write me at:

Sean Covey
Franklin Covey Co.
2200 West Parkway Boulevard
Salt Lake City, UT 84119

I would love to put you in the new book I'm planning on writing. I'm sure there are many teens out there that could learn a lot from your experience. I look forward to hearing from you!

January 1

Take me, train me, be firm with me, and I will place the world at your feet. Be easy with me and I will destroy you.

Who am I?

I am Habit.

January 2

Depending on what they are, our habits will either make us or break us. We become what we repeatedly do.

p. 8*

*All page references are to *The 7 Habits of Highly Effective Teens*.

January 3

Sow a thought, and you reap an act;
Sow an act, and you reap a habit;
Sow a habit, and you reap a character;
Sow a character, and you reap a destiny.

—SAMUEL SMILES

p. 8

January 4

Luckily, you are stronger than your habits. Therefore, you can change them. For example, try folding your arms. Now try folding them in the opposite way. How does this feel? Pretty strange, doesn't it? But if you folded them in the opposite way for thirty days in a row, it wouldn't feel so strange. You wouldn't even have to think about it. You'd get in the habit.

pp. 8–9

January 5

The 7 Habits can help you:

- Get control of your life
- Improve your relationships with your friends
- Make smarter decisions
- Get along with your parents
- Overcome addiction
- Define your values and what matters most to you
- Get more done in less time
- Increase your self-confidence
- Be happy
- Find balance between school, work, friends, and everything else

p. 9

January 6

Another word for perceptions is *paradigms* [pair-a-dimes]. A paradigm is the way you see something, your point of view, frame of reference, or belief. As you may have noticed, our paradigms are often way off the mark, and, as a result, they create limitations. For instance, you may be convinced that you don't have what it takes to get into college. But, remember, Ptolemy was just as convinced that the earth was the center of the universe.

p. 13

January 7

Paradigms are like glasses. When you have incomplete paradigms about yourself or life in general, it's like wearing glasses with the wrong prescription. That lens affects how you see everything else. As a result, what you see is what you get. If you believe you're dumb, that very belief will make you dumb. On the other hand, if you believe you're smart, that belief will cast a rosy hue on everything you do.

p. 13

January 8

Just as negative self-paradigms can put limitations on us, positive self-paradigms can bring out the best in us.

pp. 14–15

January 9

You may be wondering, "If my paradigm of myself is all contorted, what can I do to fix it?" One way is to spend time with someone who believes in you and builds you up. My mother was such a person to me. She was always saying stuff like "Sean, of course you should run for class president" and "Ask her out. I'm sure she would just die to go out with you." Whenever I needed to be affirmed I'd talk to my mom and she'd clean my glasses.

p. 15

January 10

Ask any successful person and most will tell you that they had a person who believed in them . . . a teacher, a friend, a parent, a guardian, a sister, a grandmother. It only takes one person, and it doesn't really matter who it is.

p. 16

January 11

Don't be afraid to lean on and get nourished by this person who believes in you. Go to him or her for advice. Try to see yourself the way he or she sees you. As someone once said, "If you could envision the type of person God intended you to be, you would rise up and never be the same again."

p. 16

January 12

We have paradigms not only about ourselves, but also about other people. And they can be way out of whack too. Seeing things from a different point of view can help us understand why other people act the way they do. We too often judge people without having all the facts.

p. 16

January 13

A teen named Monica had this experience:

I used to live in California, where I had a lot of good friends. I didn't care about anybody new because I already had my friends and I thought that new people should deal with it in their own way. Then, when I moved, I was the new kid and wished that someone would care about me and make me part of their group of friends. I see things in a very different way now. I know what it feels like to not have any friends.

From now on Monica will treat new kids on the block very differently, don't you think? Seeing things from another point of view can make such a difference in our attitude toward others.

p. 17

If you'd like to submit your own story about applying the 7 Habits in your life for possible future publications, e-mail your story to us at 7Hteen@7Habits.com

January 14

Our paradigms are often incomplete, inaccurate, or completely messed up. Therefore, we shouldn't be so quick to judge, label, or form rigid opinions of others, or ourselves for that matter. From our limited points of view, we seldom see the whole picture, or have all the facts.

p. 18

January 15

We should open our minds and hearts to new information, ideas, and points of view, and be willing to change our paradigms when it becomes clear that they are wrong.

p. 18

January 16

It is obvious that if we want to make big changes in our lives, the key is to change our paradigms, or the glasses through which we see the world. Change the lens and everything else follows.

p. 18

January 17

If you'll look closely, you'll find that most of your problems (with relationships, self-image, attitude) are the result of a messed-up paradigm or two. For instance, if you have a poor relationship with, say, your dad, it's likely that both of you have a warped paradigm of each other. You may see him as being totally out of touch with the modern world, and he may see you as a spoiled, ungrateful brat. In reality, both of your paradigms are probably incomplete and are holding you back from real communication.

p. 18

January 18

Besides having paradigms about ourselves and others, we also have paradigms about the world in general. You can usually tell what your paradigm is by asking yourself, "What is the driving force of my life?" "What do I spend my time thinking about?" "Who or what is my obsession?" Whatever is most important to you will become your paradigm, your glasses, or, as I like to call it, your life-center.

p. 18

January 19

Some of the more popular life-centers for teens include Friends, Stuff, Enemies, Self, and Work. They each have their good points, but they are all incomplete in one way or another, and they'll mess you up if you center your life on any one of them to the exclusion of the others.

p. 18

January 20

There's nothing better than belonging to a great group of friends and nothing worse than feeling like an outcast. Friends are important but should never become your center. Why? Well, occasionally they're fickle. Now and then they're fake. Sometimes they talk behind your back or develop new friendships and forget yours. They have mood swings. They move.

In addition, if you base your identity on having friends, being accepted, and being popular, you may find yourself compromising your standards or changing them every weekend to accommodate your friends.

Believe it or not, the day will come when friends will not be the biggest thing in your life.

p. 19

January 21

Make as many friends as you can, but don't build your life on them alone. It's an unstable foundation.

p. 19

January 22

Sometimes we see the world through the lens of possessions or "stuff." We live in a material world that teaches us that "He who dies with the most toys wins." We have to have the fastest car, the nicest clothes, the latest stereo, the best hairstyle, and the many other *things* that are supposed to bring us happiness. Possessions also come in the form of titles and accomplishments, such as head cheerleader, lead in the play, valedictorian, student body officer, chief editor, or MVP.

There is nothing wrong with accomplishments and enjoying our stuff, but we should never center our lives on *things,* which in the end have no lasting value.

p. 19

January 23

Our confidence needs to come from within, not from without, from the *quality of our hearts*, not the *quantity of things* we own. After all, he who dies with the most toys . . . still dies.

pp. 19–20

January 24

I read a saying once that says it better than I can: "If who I am is what I have and what I have is lost, then who am I?"

p. 20

January 25

Independence is more attractive than dependence. Believe me, you'll be a better boyfriend or girlfriend if you're not centered on your partner. Besides, centering your life on another doesn't show that you love them, only that you're dependent on them.

p. 21

January 26

Our education is vital to our future and should be a top priority. But we must be careful not to let dean's lists, GPAs, and AP classes take over our lives. School-centered teens often become so obsessed with getting good grades that they forget that the real purpose of school is to learn.

As thousands of teens have proved, you can do extremely well in school and still maintain a healthy balance in life. Thank goodness our worth isn't measured by our GPA.

pp. 21–22

January 27

The list of possible life-centers could go on and on: heroes, work, one's self, and even one's enemies can all become life-centers. Yet, all these and many more life-centers do not provide the stability that you and I need in life. I'm not saying we shouldn't strive to become excellent in something like dance or debate, or strive to develop outstanding relationships with our friends and parents. We should. But there's a fine line between having a passion for something and basing your entire existence on it. And that's a line we shouldn't cross.

p. 23

January 28

There is a life-center that actually works. What is it? It's being *principle-centered*.

p. 24

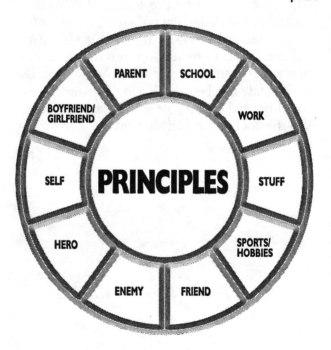

January 29

What is a principle?

We are all familiar with the effects of gravity. Throw a ball up and it comes down. It's a natural law or *principle*. Just as there are principles that rule the physical world, there are principles that rule the human world. Principles aren't religious. They aren't American or Chinese. They aren't yours or mine. They apply equally to everyone, rich or poor, king or peasant, female or male. They can't be bought or sold.

Here are a few examples of principles: honesty, service, love, hard work, respect, gratitude, moderation, fairness, integrity, loyalty, and responsibility. There are dozens and dozens more. They are not hard to identify. Just as a compass always point to true north your heart will recognize true principles.

p. 24

January 30

If you live by them, you will excel. If you break them, you will fail. It's that simple.

p. 24

January 31

Hard work is an especially important principle. There's no shortcut for hard work. You can't fake playing golf, tuning a guitar, or speaking Arabic if you haven't paid the price to get good. As the NBA great Larry Bird put it, "If you don't do your homework, you won't make your free throws."

pp. 24–25

February 1

It takes faith to live by principles, especially when you see people close to you get ahead in life by lying, cheating, indulging, manipulating, and serving only themselves. What you don't see, however, is that breaking principles always catches up with them in the end.

p. 25

February 2

Principles will never fail you. They will never talk behind your back. They don't get up and move. They don't suffer career-ending injuries. They don't play favorites based on skin color, gender, wealth, or body features. A principle-centered life is simply the most stable, immovable, unshakable foundation you can build upon, and we all need one of those.

p. 26

February 3

To grasp why principles always work, just imagine living a life based on their opposites—a life of dishonesty, loafing, indulgence, ingratitude, selfishness, and hate. I can't imagine any good thing coming out of that. Can you?

p. 26

February 4

Ironically, putting principles first is the key to doing better in all the other life-centers. If you live the principles of service, respect, and love, for instance, you're likely to pick up more friends and be a more stable boyfriend or girlfriend. Putting principles first is also the key to becoming a person of character.

p. 26

February 5

Decide today to make principles your life-center, or paradigm. In whatever situation you find yourself, ask, "What is the principle in play here?" For every problem, search for the principle that will solve it.

p. 26

February 6

BABY STEPS

1. The next time you look in the mirror say something positive about yourself.

2. Think of a limiting paradigm you might have of yourself, such as "I'm not outgoing." Now, do something today that totally contradicts that paradigm.

3. Think of a loved one or close friend who has been acting out of character lately. Consider what might be causing them to act that way.

4. The Golden Rule rules! Begin today to treat others as you would want them to treat you. Don't be impatient, complain about leftovers, or bad-mouth someone, unless you want the same treatment.

5. Sometime soon, find a quiet place where you can be alone. Think about what matters most to you.

p. 28

February 7

"The real tragedy is the tragedy of the man who never in his life braces himself for his one supreme effort—he never stretches to his full capacity, never stands up to his full stature."

—ARNOLD BENNETT

p. 32

February 8

We crawl before we walk. We learn arithmetic before algebra. We must fix ourselves before we can fix others. If you want to make a change in your life, the place to begin is with yourself, not with your parents, or your boyfriend, or your professor. All change begins with you. It's inside out. Not outside in.

p. 33

February 9

How you feel about yourself is like a bank account. Let's call it your *Personal Bank Account* (PBA). Just like a checking or savings account at a bank, you can make deposits into and take withdrawals from your PBA by the things you think, say, and do. For example, when I stick to a commitment I've made to myself, I feel in control. It's a deposit. *Cha-ching.* On the other hand, when I break a promise to myself, I feel disappointed and make a withdrawal.

p. 34

February 10

How is your PBA? How much trust and confidence do you have in yourself? Are you loaded or bankrupt? Take time to think about it.

p. 34

February 11

Possible symptoms of a poor Personal Bank Account:

- You cave in to peer pressure easily.

- You wrestle with feelings of depression and inferiority.

- You're overly concerned about what others think of you.

- You act arrogant to help hide your insecurities.

- You self-destruct by getting heavily into drugs, vandalism, or gangs.

- You get jealous easily, especially when someone close to you succeeds.

p. 34

February 12

Possible symptoms of a healthy Personal Bank Account:

- You stand up for yourself and resist peer pressure.
- You're not overly concerned about being popular.
- You see life as a generally positive experience.
- You trust yourself.
- You are goal-driven.
- You are happy for the success of others.

p. 34

February 13

If your Personal Bank Account is low, don't get discouraged about it. Just start today by making $1, $5, $10, or $25 deposits. Eventually you'll get your confidence back. Small deposits over a long period of time is the way to a healthy and rich PBA.

p. 35

February 14

Here are six key deposits that can help you build your PBA. Of course, with every deposit, there is an equal and opposite withdrawal.

PBA DEPOSITS	PBA WITHDRAWALS
Keep promises to yourself	Break personal promises
Do small acts of kindness	Keep to yourself
Be gentle with yourself	Beat yourself up
Be honest	Be dishonest
Renew yourself	Wear yourself out
Tap into your talents	Neglect your talents

p. 35

February 15

Have you ever had friends or roommates who seldom come through? They say they'll call you and they don't. They promise to pick you up for the game and they forget. After a while, you don't trust them. Their commitments mean nothing. The same thing occurs when you continually make and break promises to yourself, such as "I'm going to get up at six tomorrow morning" or "I'm going to get my homework done right when I get home." After a while you don't trust yourself.

p. 35

February 16

We should treat the commitments we make to ourselves as seriously as those we make to the most important people in our lives.

p. 35

February 17

If you're feeling out of control in life, focus on the single thing you can control—yourself. Make a promise to yourself and keep it. Start with real small $10 commitments that you know you can complete, like committing to eat healthier today. After you've built up some self-trust, you can then go for the more difficult $100 deposits, such as deciding to end an unhealthy relationship or not going after your sister for wearing your new clothes.

p. 35

February 18

I remember reading a statement by a psychiatrist who said that if you ever feel depressed, the best thing to do is to do something for someone else. Why? Because it gets you focused outward, not inward. It's hard to be depressed while serving someone else. Ironically, a by-product of helping others is feeling wonderful yourself.

pp. 35–36

February 19

Go out of your way to say hello to the loneliest person you know. Write a thank-you note to someone who has made a difference in your life, like a friend, teacher, or coach. The next time you're at a tollbooth, pay for the car behind you. Giving gives life not only to others but also to yourself.

p. 37

February 20

I love these lines from *The Man Nobody Knows* by Bruce Barton, which illustrate that giving to others is like giving to yourself as well:

> There are two seas in Palestine. One is fresh, and fish are in it. Splashes of green adorn its banks. Trees spread their branches over it and stretch out their thirsty roots to sip of its healing waters. . . . The River Jordan makes this sea with sparkling water from the hills. So it laughs in the sunshine. And men build their houses near to it, and birds their nests; and every kind of life is happier because it is there.

> The River Jordan flows on south into another sea.

> Here is no splash of fish, no fluttering leaf, no song of birds, no children's laughter. Travelers choose another route, unless on urgent business. The air hangs heavy above its water, and neither man nor beast nor fowl will drink.

> What makes this mighty difference in these neighbor seas? Not the River Jordan. It empties the same good water into both. Not the soil in which they lie; not in the country round about.

> This is the difference. The Sea of Galilee receives but does not keep the Jordan. For every drop that flows into it another drop flows out. The giving and receiving go on in equal measure. The other sea is shrewder, hoarding its income jealously. It will not be tempted into any generous impulse. Every drop it gets, it keeps.

The Sea of Galilee gives and lives. This other sea gives nothing. It is named the Dead.

There are two kinds of people in this world. There are two seas in Palestine.

p. 37

February 21

Be gentle with yourself. Don't expect yourself to be perfect by tomorrow morning. If you're a late bloomer, and many of us are, be patient and give yourself time to grow.

p. 37

February 22

Being gentle with yourself also means learning to laugh at the stupid things you do and forgiving yourself when you mess up. We should learn from our mistakes, but we shouldn't beat the tar out of ourselves over them. The past is just that, past. Learn what went wrong and why. Make amends if you need to. Then drop it and move on. Throw that voodoo doll out with the trash.

p. 38

February 23

"One of the keys to happiness is a bad memory."

—RITA MAE BROWN

p. 38

February 24

A ship at sea for many years picks up thousands of barnacles that attach themselves to the bottom of the ship and eventually weigh it down, becoming a threat to its safety. Such a ship ultimately needs its barnacles removed, and the least expensive and easiest way is for the ship to harbor in a freshwater port, free of salt water. Soon the barnacles become loose on their own and fall off. The ship is then able to return to sea, relieved of its burden.

Are you carrying around barnacles in the form of mistakes, regrets, and pain from the past? Perhaps you need to allow yourself to soak in fresh water for a while. Letting go of a burden and giving yourself a second chance may just be the deposit you need right now.

p. 38

February 25

Be honest, starting with yourself. Whenever we are fake and try to be something we're not, we feel unsure of ourselves and make a PBA withdrawal. I love how Judy Garland put it: "Always be a first-rate version of yourself, instead of a second-rate version of somebody else."

p. 38

February 26

Be honest in your actions. Are you honest at school, with your parents, and with your boss? If you've been dishonest in the past, and I think we all have, try being honest and notice how whole it makes you feel. Remember, you can't do wrong and feel right.

p. 39

February 27

Every act of honesty is a deposit into your PBA and will build strength. As the saying goes, "My strength is as the strength of ten because my heart is pure."

p. 39

February 28

Honesty is always the best policy, even when it's not the trend.

p. 39

February 29

Renew yourself. You've got to take time for yourself, to renew and to relax. If you don't, you'll lose your zest for life.

p. 39

March 1

We all need a place we can escape to, a sanctuary of some sort, where we can renew our spirits. And it doesn't have to be a rose garden, mountaintop, or beachfront. It can be a bedroom, or even a bathroom, just a peaceful place to be alone.

p. 40

March 2

Besides finding a place of refuge, there are so many other ways to renew yourself and build your PBA. Exercise can do it, like going for a walk, running, dancing, or punching a bag. How about watching old movies, playing a musical instrument, finger painting, or talking to friends who uplift you?

p. 41

March 3

Finding and then developing a talent, hobby, or special interest can be one of the single greatest deposits you can make into your PBA.

p. 41

March 4

Talents come in a variety of packages (not just the high-profile ones). Don't think small. You may have a knack for reading, writing, or speaking. You may have a gift for being creative, being a fast learner, or being accepting of others. You may have organizational, music, or leadership skills. It doesn't matter where your talent may lie, whether it's in chess, drama, or butterfly collecting, when you do something you like doing and have a talent for—it's exhilarating. It's a form of self-expression and it builds esteem.

p. 41

March 5

BABY STEPS

1. Get up when you planned to for three days in a row.

2. Identify one easy task that needs to be done today, like putting in a batch of laundry, or reading a book for an English assignment. Decide when you will do it. Now, keep your word and get it done.

3. Sometime today, do a kind anonymous deed, like writing a kind note, taking out the trash, or making someone's bed.

4. Look around and find something you can do to make a difference, like cleaning up a park in your neighborhood, volunteering in a senior citizens center, or reading to someone who can't.

5. Think of a talent you would like to develop this year. Write down specific steps to get there.

p. 45

March 6

MORE BABY STEPS

1. Try to go an entire day without negative self-talk. Each time you catch yourself putting yourself down, you have to replace it with three positive thoughts about yourself.

2. Decide on a fun activity that will lift your spirits and do it today. For example, turn up the music and dance.

3. The next time your parents ask you about what you're doing, share the complete story. Don't mislead or deceive by leaving out information.

4. For one day, try not to exaggerate or embellish.

p. 46

March 7

Habit 1 is Be Proactive. It is the key to unlocking all of the other habits and that's why it comes first. Habit 1 says, "I am the force. I am the captain of my life. I can choose my attitude. I'm responsible for my own happiness or unhappiness. I am in the driver's seat of my destiny, not just a passenger."

p. 48

Reactive ▼

▲ Proactive

March 8

There are two types of people in this world—the proactive and the reactive—those who take responsibility for their lives and those who blame; those who make it happen and those who get happened to.

p. 48

March 9

"People are just about as happy as they
make up their mind to be."

—ABRAHAM LINCOLN

p. 48

March 10

Each day you and I have about 100 chances to be proactive or reactive. In any given day, the weather is bad, you can't find a job, your sister steals your blouse, you lose an election at school, your friend talks behind your back, someone calls you names, your parents don't let you take the car (for no reason), you flunk a test. So what are you going to do about it? Are you in the habit of reacting to these kinds of everyday things, or are you proactive? The choice is yours.

p. 49

March 11

Reactive people make choices based on impulse. They are like a can of soda pop. If life shakes them up a bit, the pressure builds and they suddenly explode.

p. 49

March 12

Proactive people make choices based on values. They *think* before they act. They recognize they can't control everything that happens to them, but they can control *what they do about it*.

p. 49

March 13

Unlike reactive people who are full of carbonation, proactive people are like water. Shake them up all you want, take off the lid, and nothing. No fizzing, no bubbling, no pressure. They are calm, cool, and in control.

p. 49

March 14

You can usually hear the difference between proactive and reactive people by the type of language they use. Reactive language usually sounds like this:

"That's me. That's just the way I am." What they're really saying is, *I'm not responsible for the way I act. I can't change. I was predetermined to be this way.*

"Thanks a lot. You just ruined my day." What they're really saying is, *I'm not in control of my own moods. You are.*

Notice that reactive language takes power away from you and gives it to something or someone else.

p. 51

March 15

As John Bytheway explains in his book *What I Wish I'd Known in High School*, when you're reactive it's like giving someone else the remote control to your life and saying, "Here, change my mood anytime you wish."

Proactive language, on the other hand, puts the remote control back into your own hands. You are then free to choose which channel you want to be on.

p. 51

March 16

REACTIVE LANGUAGE	PROACTIVE LANGUAGE
I'll try	I'll do it
That's just the way I am	I can do better than that
There's nothing I can do	Let's look at our options
I have to	I choose to
I can't	There's gotta be a way
You ruined my day	I'm not going to let your bad mood rub off on me

p. 51

March 17

Some people suffer from a contagious virus I call "victimitis." Perhaps you've seen it. People infected with victimitis believe that everyone has it in for them and that the world owes them something ... which isn't the case at all. I like the way author Mark Twain put it: "Don't go around saying the world owes you a living. The world owes you nothing. It was here first."

p. 52

March 18

Besides feeling like victims, reactive people:

- Are easily offended
- Blame others
- Get angry and say things they later regret
- Whine and complain
- Wait for things to happen to them
- Change only when they have to

pp. 52–53

March 19

Proactive people are a different breed. Proactive people:

- Are not easily offended

- Take responsibility for their choices

- Think before they act

- Bounce back when something bad happens

- Always find a way to make it happen

- Focus on things they can do something about, and don't worry about things they can't

p. 53

March 20

The fact is, we can't control everything that happens to us. We can't control the color of our skin, who will win the NBA finals, where we were born, who our parents are, how much tuition will be next fall, or how others might treat us. But there is one thing we *can* control: *how we respond to what happens to us.* And that is what counts! This is why we need to stop worrying about things we can't control and start worrying about things we *can.*

p. 54

March 21

Proactive people focus on the things they *can* control. By doing so they experience inner peace and gain more control of their lives. They learn to smile about and live with the many things they can't do anything about. They may not like them, but they know it's no use worrying.

p. 56

March 22

Life often deals us a bad hand and it is up to us to control how we respond. Every time we have a setback, it's an opportunity for us to turn it into a triumph.

p. 56

March 23

Bad habits such as abuse and alcoholism are often passed down from parents to kids, and as a result, dysfunctional families keep repeating themselves. The good news is that you can stop the cycle. Because you are proactive, you can stop these bad habits from being passed on. You can become a "change agent" and pass on good habits to future generations, starting with your own kids.

pp. 59–60

March 24

You have the power within you to rise above whatever has been passed down to you. No matter how bad your predicament is, you can become a change agent and create a new life for yourself.

p. 61

March 25

Being proactive really means two things. First, you take responsibility for your life. Second, you have a "can-do" attitude. "Can-do" is very different from "no-can-do." Just take a peek:

CAN-DO PEOPLE	NO-CAN-DO PEOPLE
Take initiative to make it happen	Wait for something to happen to them
Think about solutions and options	Think about problems and barriers
Act	Are acted upon

p. 63

March 26

To reach your goals in life, you must seize the initiative. If you're feeling bad about not being asked out on dates, for instance, don't just sit around and sulk. Do something about it! Find ways to meet people. Be friendly and try smiling a lot. Ask *them* out. They may not know how great you are.

p. 63

March 27

Don't wait for that perfect job to fall in your lap, go after it. Send out your résumé, network, volunteer to work for free.

p. 64

March 28

Some people mistake a can-do attitude for being pushy, aggressive, or obnoxious. Wrong. Can-do is courageous, persistent, and smart. Others think can-do people stretch the rules and make their own laws. Not so. Can-do thinkers are creative, enterprising, and extremely resourceful.

p. 64

March 29

George Bernard Shaw, the English playwright, knew all about can-do. Listen to how he said it: "People are always blaming their circumstances for what they are. I don't believe in circumstances. The people who get on in this world are the people who get up and look for the circumstances they want, and if they can't find them, make them."

p. 65

March 30

When someone is rude to you, where do you get the power to resist being rude back? For starters, *just push pause*. Yep, just reach up and push the pause button to your life just as you would on your remote control. (If I remember right, the pause button is found somewhere in the middle of your forehead.) Sometimes life is moving so fast that we instantly react to everything out of sheer habit. If you can learn to pause, get control, and think about how you want to respond, you'll make smarter decisions.

pp. 65–66

March 31

BABY STEPS

1. The next time someone flips you off, give him or her the peace sign back.

2. Listen carefully to your words today. Count how many times you use reactive language, such as "You make me . . ." "I have to . . ." "Why can't they . . ."

3. Do something today that you have wanted to do but never dared. Leave your comfort zone and go for it. Ask someone out on a date, raise your hand in class, or join a team.

4. Write yourself a Post-it note: "I will not let _____ decide how I'm going to feel." Place it in your locker, on your mirror, or in your planner and refer to it often.

p. 71

April 1

MORE BABY STEPS

1. At the next party, don't just sit against the wall and wait for excitement to find you, you find it. Walk up and introduce yourself to someone new.

2. The next time you receive a grade that you think is unfair, don't blow it off or cry about it, make an appointment with the teacher to discuss it and then see what you can learn.

3. If you get in a fight with a parent or a friend, be the first to apologize.

p. 71

April 2

Habit 2, Begin with the End in Mind, means developing a clear picture of where you want to go with your life. It means deciding what your values are and setting goals. Habit 1 says you are the driver of your life, not the passenger. Habit 2 says, since you're the driver, decide where you want to go and draw up a map to get there.

p. 74

April 3

You've just been asked to put together a jigsaw puzzle. Having done many such puzzles, you're excited to get started. You pour out all 1,000 pieces, spreading them out across a large table. You then pick up the lid to the box and look at what you're putting together. But there's no picture! It's blank! How will you ever be able to finish the puzzle without knowing what it looks like, you wonder? If you only had a one-second glimpse of what it's supposed to be. That's what you need. What a difference it would make! Without it, you don't have a clue where to even start.

Now think about your own life and your 1,000 pieces. Do you have an end in mind? Do you have a clear picture of who you want to be one year from now? Or are you clueless?

p. 74

April 4

By saying Begin with the End in Mind, I'm not talking about deciding every little detail of your future, like choosing your career or deciding who you'll marry. I'm simply talking about thinking beyond today and deciding where you want to take your life, so that each step you take is always in the right direction.

p. 74

April 5

Why is it so important to have an end in mind? I'll give you two good reasons. The first is that you are at a critical crossroads in life, and the paths you choose now can affect you forever. The second is that if you don't decide your own future, someone else will do it for you.

p. 76

April 6

So here you are. You're young. You're free. You have your whole life before you. You're standing at the crossroads of life and you have to choose which paths to take.

- Do you want to go to college or graduate school?

- What will your attitude toward life be?

- What type of friends do you want to have?

- Who will you date?

- What values will you choose?

- What kind of relationships do you want with your family?

p. 76

April 7

Imagine an eighty-foot rope stretched out before you. Each foot represents one year of your life. Teenagehood is only seven years, such a short span of rope, but those seven affect the remaining sixty-one for good or bad, in such a powerful way.

p. 76

April 8

Friends can have a powerful influence on your attitude, reputation, and direction. The need to be accepted and be part of a group is powerful. But too often we choose our friends based on whoever will accept us. And that's not always good. For example, to be accepted by the kids who do drugs, all you have to do is do drugs yourself. It's hard, but sometimes it is better to have no friends for a time than to have the wrong friends.

pp. 76–77

April 9

What about sex? Talk about an important decision with huge consequences! If you wait until the "heat of the moment" to choose which path to take, it's too late. Your decision has already been made. You need to decide now. The path you choose will affect your health, your self-image, how fast you grow up, and your reputation.

p. 78

April 10

In a recent poll, going to movies was ranked as the favorite pastime of teens. We all love movies, but be careful about the values they promote. The movies lie, especially when it comes to issues like sex. They glamorize sleeping around and having one-night stands without acknowledging the potential risks and consequences.

p. 78

April 11

We are free to choose our paths, but we can't choose the consequences that come with them. Have you ever gone water sliding? You can choose which slide you want to go down, but once you're sliding, you can't very well stop. You must live with the consequences . . . to the end.

p. 78

April 12

Without an end of our own in mind we are often so quick to follow anyone who is willing to lead, even into things that won't get us far.

p. 80

April 13

The best way to begin with the end in mind is to write a Personal Mission Statement. A Personal Mission Statement is like a personal credo or motto that states what your life is about. It is like the blueprint to your life. Countries have constitutions, which function just like a mission statement. And most companies, like Microsoft and Coca-Cola, have mission statements. But they work best with people.

p. 81

April 14

So, why not write your own personal mission statement? Many teens have. Mission statements come in all types and varieties. Some are long, some are short. Some are poems and some are songs. Some teens have used their favorite quote as a mission statement. Others have used a picture or a photograph.

p. 81

April 15

This mission statement was written by a teen named Katie Hall. It is short, but to her it means everything:

My Mission Statement

NOTHING

LESS

p. 91

April 16

A Personal Mission Statement is like a tree with deep roots. It is stable and isn't going anywhere, but it is also alive and continually growing.

p. 83

April 17

An important part of developing a Personal Mission Statement is discovering what you're good at. Everyone has a talent, a gift, something that they do well. Some talents, like having the singing voice of an angel, attract a lot of attention. But there are many other talents, maybe not as attention-grabbing but every bit as important if not more— things like being skilled at listening, making people laugh, forgiving, drawing, or just being nice.

pp. 83–84

April 18

We all blossom at different times. So if you're a late bloomer, relax. It may take you a while to uncover your talents. Viktor Frankl, a famous Jewish-Austrian psychiatrist who survived the death camps of Nazi Germany, taught that we don't *invent* our talents in life but rather we *detect* them. In other words, you are already born with your talents, you just need to uncover them.

p. 84

April 19

Once you have written your Personal Mission Statement, put it in a place where you can easily access it, like inside your journal or on your mirror. Or you could reduce it, laminate it, and put it in your purse or wallet. Then refer to it often, or, even better, memorize it.

p. 91

April 20

In order to live by your mission statement, you have to set goals for yourself. Goals are more specific than a mission statement. If your personal mission were to eat a whole pizza, your goal would be how to slice it up. Don't go on a guilt trip when you hear the word *goals*. Forget about any mistakes you may have made in the past. Follow the advice of George Bernard Shaw, who said: "When I was a young man, I observed that nine out of ten things I did were failures. I didn't want to be a failure, so I did ten times more work."

p. 94

April 21

How many times do we set goals when we are in the mood but then later find we don't have the strength to follow through? Why does this happen? It's because we haven't *counted the cost* of reaching those goals.

p. 94

April 22

Let's say you set a goal to get better grades in school this year. Great. But now, before you begin, count the cost. What will it require? For instance, you will have to spend more time doing math and grammar and less time hanging out with your friends. You will have to stay up late some nights. Finding time for schoolwork might mean giving up watching TV or reading your favorite magazine.

Now, having counted the cost, consider the benefits. What could good grades bring you? A feeling of accomplishment? A scholarship to college? A good job? Now ask yourself, "Am I willing to make the sacrifice?"

p. 94

April 23

Make a goal bite-sized. Instead of setting a goal to get better grades in all your classes, you might set a goal to get better grades in just two classes. Then, next semester, take another bite.

pp. 94–95

April 24

It's been said, "A goal not written is only a wish." There are no ifs and buts about it, a written goal carries ten times the power.

p. 95

April 25

"If you do the thing," said Ralph Waldo Emerson, "you will have the power." Each time you commit yourself to a goal, you will dig up gold mines of willpower, skill, and creativity you never thought you possessed. Those who are committed always find a way.

p. 96

April 26

Certain moments in life contain momentum and power. The key is to harness these moments for goal setting. Things with starts and finishes or beginnings and ends carry momentum. For example, a new year represents a start. Breaking up with someone, on the other hand, represents an end. Here is a list of moments that can provide momentum for you as you set out to make new goals:

- A setback
- Moving to a new city
- A new job
- A new season
- A triumph
- Death
- Graduation
- A demotion
- A life-changing experience

p. 97

April 27

Are you familiar with the myth of the phoenix bird? After every lifespan of 500 years, the beautiful phoenix would burn itself at the stake. Out of the ashes, it would later arise, reborn. In like manner, we can regenerate ourselves out of the ashes of a bad experience. Setbacks and tragedies can often serve as a springboard for change.

pp. 97–98

April 28

Sticking with something when you don't feel like it is the true test of your character. As someone once put it:

Character is the discipline to follow through with the resolutions long after the spirit in which they were made has passed.

p. 98

April 29

You'll accomplish more in life if you borrow strength from others. Mountain climbers "rope up": they tie themselves together with ropes to aid them in climbing and to save lives if one person were to fall. You can also "rope up" in life—with friends, brothers, sisters, girlfriends, parents, counselors, grandparents, pastors. The more ropes you have out, the greater your chances for success.

p. 98

April 30

People who lack the native physical, social, or mental gifts they desire must fight just that much harder. And that uphill battle can produce qualities and strengths they couldn't develop any other way. That is how a weakness can become a strength. So if you're not endowed with all the beauty, biceps, bucks, or brains that you covet—congratulations! You just may have the better draw.

p. 102

May 1

Good timber does not grow with ease,
The stronger wind, the stronger trees.

—FROM A POEM BY DOUGLAS MALLOCH

p. 102

May 2

Life is a mission, not a career. A career is a profession. A mission is a cause. A career asks, "What's in it for me?" A mission asks, "How can I make a difference?"

p. 103

May 3

You don't have to change the world to have a mission. As educator Maren Mouritsen says, "Most of us will never do great things. But we can do small things in a great way."

p. 103

May 4

BABY STEPS

1. Review your mission statement daily for thirty days (that's how long it takes to develop a habit). Let it guide you in all your decisions.

2. Ask yourself, "Would I want to marry someone like me?" If not, work to develop the qualities you're lacking.

3. Think about your goals. Have you put them in pen and written them down?

4. Identify a negative label others may have given you. Think up a few things you can do to change that label.

p. 104

May 5

Habit 3 is Put First Things First. It's all about learning to prioritize and manage your time so that your first things come first, not last. But putting first things first also deals with learning to overcome your fears and being strong during hard moments.

p. 106

May 6

Have you ever packed a suitcase and noticed how much more you can fit inside when you neatly fold and organize your clothes instead of just throwing them in? It's really quite surprising. The same goes for your life. The better you organize yourself, the more you'll be able to pack in—more time for family and friends, more time for school, more time for yourself, more time for your first things.

p. 107

May 7

Use a planner of some sort that has a calendar and space to write down appointments, assignments, to-do lists, and goals. You can even make your own planner out of a spiral-bound notebook. Planners come in all sizes, so choose one that's most convenient for you.

pp. 112–13

May 8

Plan weekly. Take fifteen minutes each week to plan your week and just watch what a difference it can make.

p. 113

May 9

At the beginning or end of each week, sit down and think about what you want to accomplish for the upcoming week. Think of the most important things you have to do as big rocks (examples: study for a chemistry test, finish reading a book, complete employment application, exercise three times). Think of all the little everyday things you have to do as pebbles (examples: chores, busywork, phone calls).

Have you ever seen the big-rock experiment? You fill a bucket half full of pebbles and then put several big rocks on top of the pebbles. They don't all fit. But if you start over and put the big rocks in the bucket first and then the pebbles, everything fits. The pebbles neatly fit in the spaces around the big rocks.

Think of your schedule in terms of big rocks and pebbles. First book your big rocks and then schedule in all of your other little to-dos.

pp. 114–15

May 10

With your weekly plan in place, adapt each day as needed. You'll probably need to rearrange some big rocks and pebbles now and then. Try your best to follow your plan, but if you don't accomplish everything you set out to do, no big deal. Even if you only get a third of your big rocks accomplished, that's a third more than you might have accomplished without planning ahead.

pp. 115–16

May 11

One of the few things that can't be recycled is wasted time. So make sure you treasure each moment. In the words of Queen Elizabeth I on her deathbed: "All my possessions for one moment of time."

p. 116

May 12

It takes guts to stay true to your first things, like your values and standards, when the pressure is on. Staying true to your first things will often cause you to stretch outside your comfort zone.

p. 117

May 13

Your comfort zone represents things you're familiar with, places you know, friends you're at ease with, activities you enjoy doing. Your comfort zone is risk-free. On the other hand, things like making new friends, speaking before a large audience, or sticking up for your values makes your hair stand on end. Welcome to the courage zone!

p. 117

May 14

Everything that makes us feel uncomfortable is in the courage zone. In this territory waits uncertainty, pressure, change, the possibility of failure. But it's also the place to go for opportunity and the only place in which you'll ever reach your full potential. You'll never reach it by hanging out in your comfort zone, that's for sure.

p. 117

May 15

Nothing is wrong with enjoying your comfort zone. In fact, much of your time should be spent there. But you know that people who seldom try new things or spread their wings live safe but boring lives!

p. 118

May 16

"You miss 100 percent of the shots you never take."

—WAYNE GRETZKY

p. 118

May 17

There are a lot of unhelpful emotions in this world, but perhaps one of the worst is *fear*. When I think about all I failed to do in my life because my fears got the best of me I ache inside. Throughout my life there have been classes I never took, friends I never made, and teams I never played for—all because of these ugly, yet very real fears

p. 118

May 18

Our doubts are traitors,
And make us lose the good we oft might win
By fearing to attempt.

—WILLIAM SHAKESPEARE, *Measure for Measure*

May 19

Think of all the heroic acts that have been accomplished by people who acted in the face of fear. Think of Nelson Mandela, Susan B. Anthony, Winston Churchill, Martin Luther King, Jr.

pp. 118–19

May 20

As Edmund Hillary, the first person to climb Mount Everest and live to tell about it, put it, "It's not the mountain we conquer, but ourselves."

pp. 120–21

May 21

The next time you want to

- make a new friend,

- resist peer pressure,

- break an old habit,

- develop a new skill,

- try out for a team,

- audition for a play,

- ask someone out,

- get involved,

- be yourself,

or even sing in public . . . Do it! . . . even when all your fears and doubts scream out, "You stink," "You'll fail," "Don't try."

p. 121

May 22

Never let your fears make your decisions. You make them.

p. 121

May 23

One way I've learned to overcome fear is to keep this thought always in the back of my mind: *Winning is nothing more than rising each time you fall.*

p. 121

May 24

Hard moments are conflicts between doing the right thing and doing the easier thing. Small hard moments occur daily and include things like getting up when your alarm rings, controlling your temper, or disciplining yourself to do your homework. Large hard moments occur every so often in life and include things like choosing good friends, resisting negative peer pressure, and rebounding after a major setback. These moments have huge consequences and strike when you're least expecting them. If you recognize that these moments will come (and they will), then you can prepare for them and meet them head-on like a warrior and come out victorious.

p. 122

May 25

Be courageous at key junctures! Don't sacrifice your future happiness for one night of pleasure, a weekend of excitement, or a thrilling moment of revenge.

p. 122

May 26

If you are ever thinking about doing something really stupid, remember these lines from Shakespeare:

> *What win I, if I gain the thing I seek?*
> *A dream, a breath, a froth of fleeting joy.*
> *Who buys a minute's mirth to wail a week?*
> *Or sells eternity to get a toy?*
> *For one sweet grape who will the vine destroy?*

These lines are about sacrificing your future for a brief moment of joy.

p. 123

May 27

Saying no when all your friends are saying yes takes raw courage. However, standing up to peer pressure, what I call "won't power," is a massive deposit into your PBA.

p. 123

May 28

To overcome peer pressure, you've got to care more about what *you* think of you than what *your peers* think of you.

p. 124

May 29

Not all peer pressure is bad. In fact, much of it can be very good. If you can find a friend who puts positive pressure on you to be your best, then hang on to him or her for dear life, because you've got something very special.

p. 125

May 30

If you find yourself wanting to stand up but instead you are continually caving in to peer pressure, the first thing to do is build your PBA. If your self-confidence and self-respect are low, how can you expect to have the strength to resist? Make a promise to yourself and keep it. Help somebody in need. Develop a talent. Renew yourself. Eventually you'll have sufficient strength to forge your own path instead of following the beaten ones.

p. 125

May 31

If you haven't decided what your values are, how can you expect to stick up for them?

p. 125

June 1

Albert E. Gray's Common Denominator of Success:

> *All successful people have the habit of doing the things failures don't like to do. They don't like doing them either necessarily. But their disliking is subordinated to the strength of their purpose.*

What he means is successful people are willing to suck it up from time to time and do things they don't like doing. Why do they do them? Because they know these things will lead them to their goals.

pp. 125–26

June 2

An all-American collegiate wrestler was asked what the most memorable day of his career had been. He replied that it was the one day during his career when practice had been canceled. He hated practice, but was willing to endure it for a greater purpose, his love of being the best he could be.

p. 126

If you'd like to submit your own story about applying the 7 Habits in your life for possible future publications, e-mail your story to us at 7Hteen@7Habits.com

June 3

To realize the value of One Year,
Ask a student who failed his or her AP exams.
To realize the value of One Month
Ask a mother who gave birth to a premature baby.
To realize the value of One Week,
Ask an editor of a weekly magazine.
To realize the value of One Day,
Ask a daily wage laborer who has six kids to feed.
To realize the value of One Hour,
Ask the lovers who are waiting to meet.
To realize the value of One Minute,
Ask a person who missed their train.
To realize the value of One Second,
Ask the person who survived an accident.
To realize the value of One Millisecond,
Ask the person who won a silver medal in the
Olympics.

—UNKNOWN

p. 127

June 4

BABY STEPS

1. Set a goal to use a planner for one month. Stick to your plan.

2. Identify your biggest time-wasters. Do you really need to spend two hours on the phone, surf the Web all night, or watch that sitcom rerun?

3. Are you a "pleaser," someone who says yes to everything and everyone? If so, have the courage to say no when it's the right thing to do.

4. If you have an important test in one week, don't procrastinate and wait until the day before to study. Suck it up and study a little each day.

p. 128

June 5

MORE BABY STEPS

1. Identify a fear that is holding you back from reaching your goals. Decide right now to jump outside of your comfort zone and stop letting that fear get the best of you.

2. How much impact does peer pressure have on you? Identify the person or people who have the most influence upon you. Ask yourself, "Am I doing what I want to do or what they want me to do?"

p. 128

June 6

One of my favorite quotes is "On their deathbed nobody has ever wished they had spent more time at the office." I've often asked myself, "What *do* they wish they had spent more time doing?" I think the answer might be "Spent more time with the people they love." You see, it's all about relationships, the stuff that life is made of.

p. 131

June 7

The most important ingredient in any relationship is *what you are*. As the essayist and philosopher Ralph Waldo Emerson put it, "Who you are speaks so loudly I can't hear what you're saying." If you're struggling in your relationships, you probably don't have to look any further than yourself for the answer.

p. 132

June 8

The Personal Bank Account (PBA) represents the amount of trust and confidence you have in yourself. The Relationship Bank Account (RBA) represents the amount of trust and confidence you have in each of your relationships.

The RBA is very much like a checking account at a bank. You can make deposits and improve the relationship, or take withdrawals and weaken it. A strong and healthy relationship is always the result of steady deposits made over a long period of time.

p. 132

June 9

You have an RBA with everyone you meet. Suppose you come across a new kid in the neighborhood. If you smile and say hello, you've just opened an account with him. If you ignore him, you've just opened an account as well, although a negative one.

pp. 132–33

June 10

If you open an RBA with another person, you can never close it. That's why you can run into a friend you haven't seen in years and pick up right where you left off. It's also why people hang on to grudges for years.

p. 133

June 11

In a checking account, ten dollars is ten dollars. In an RBA, deposits tend to evaporate and withdrawals tend to turn to stone. This means that you need to continually make small deposits into your most important relationships just to keep them in the positive.

p. 133

June 12

How can you build a rich relationship or repair a broken one? It's simple. One deposit at a time. There is no quick fix. If my relationship with you is $5,000 in the hole, I'll need to make $5,001 worth of deposits to get it back in the positive.

p. 133

June 13

There are many kinds of RBA deposits, but here are six that seem to work every time:

- Keep promises
- Do small acts of kindness
- Be loyal
- Listen
- Say you're sorry
- Set clear expectations

p. 134

June 14

What is the most powerful deposit someone has made into your RBA? What are the largest deposits you have made into someone else's RBA?

p. 133

June 15

Keeping small commitments and promises is vital to building trust. You must do what you say you're going to do. If you find you can't keep a commitment for some reason (it happens), then let the other person know why.

p. 135

June 16

If your RBA with your parents is low, try building it by keeping your commitments, because when your parents trust you, everything goes so much better. (I know you already know this.)

p. 135

June 17

Have you ever had a day where everything is going wrong and you feel totally depressed . . . and then suddenly, out of nowhere, someone says something nice to you and it turns your whole day around? Sometimes the smallest things—a hello, a kind note, a smile, a compliment, a hug—can make such a big difference. If you want to build friendships, try doing the little things, because in relationships the little things *are* the big things.

pp. 135–36

June 18

"One kind word can warm three winter months."

—JAPANESE SAYING

p. 136

June 19

"I can live three months on a good compliment."

—MARK TWAIN

p. 136

June 20

Small acts of kindness don't always have to be one on one. You can also join with others to make a deposit.

p. 137

June 21

Think about what a deposit means to someone else, not what *you* would want as a deposit. A nice gift may be a deposit for you, but a listening ear may be a deposit for another person.

p. 138

June 22

If you ever have something nice to say, don't let that thought just rot, *say it!* As Ken Blanchard wrote in his book *The One Minute Manager*, "Unexpressed good thoughts aren't worth squat!" Don't wait until people are dead to give them flowers.

p. 138

June 23

One of the biggest RBA deposits you can make is to be loyal to other people, not only when they're in your presence but more especially when they're not present.

p. 138

June 24

When you talk behind people's backs, you're only hurting yourself, in two ways. First, you make withdrawals from everyone who hears your comments. Second, when you bad-mouth or gossip you make what I call an "invisible withdrawal" from the person you're attacking.

p. 138

June 25

We gossip because we're insecure, afraid, or threatened. That's why gossipers usually like to pick on people who look different, think different, are self-confident, or stand out in some way. But isn't it kind of silly to think that tearing someone else down builds you up?

p. 139

June 26

When people share something with you and ask you to keep it "just between you and me," then for goodness' sake, keep it "just between you and them" instead of running out and telling every last soul every juicy detail as if you had no control of your bodily functions. If you enjoy being told secrets, then keep them secret, and you'll get more of 'em told to you.

p. 139

June 27

Strong minds talk about ideas; weak minds talk about people.

p. 140

June 28

The next time a group starts gossiping about another person, refuse to participate in the gossip or stick up for that person. You can do so without sounding self-righteous.

p. 140

June 29

Cutting against the grain of a gossip pile-on takes courage. But after the initial embarrassment it may cause you, people will admire you because they know you're loyal to the core.

p. 140

June 30

People need to feel safe and secure in relationships, as illustrated so well in the *Winnie-the-Pooh* classics:

Piglet sidled up behind Pooh.

"Pooh," he whispered.

"Yes, Piglet?"

"Nothing," said Piglet, taking Pooh's paw. "I just wanted to be sure of you."

p. 140

July 1

Listening to someone can be one of the single greatest deposits you can make into another's RBA.

p. 140

July 2

People need to be listened to almost as much as they need food. And if you have time to feed them, you'll create some fabulous friendships.

p. 141

July 3

Saying you're sorry when you yell, overreact, or make a stupid mistake can quickly restore an overdrawn bank account.

p. 141

July 4

Apologies disarm people. When people get offended their tendency is to take up a sword, so to speak, to protect themselves in the future. But when you apologize, you take away their desire to fight you and they will drop their sword.

p. 142

July 5

Pick one important relationship in your life that is damaged. It may be with a parent or a sibling or a friend. Now commit yourself to rebuilding that relationship one deposit at a time. Remember, it may take months to build up what took months to tear down. But little by little, deposit by deposit, they'll begin to see that you are genuine.

p. 143

July 6

BABY STEPS

1. All day today, before giving out any commitments, pause and think about whether or not you can honor them. Don't say, "I'll call tonight" or, "Let's have lunch today," unless you can follow through.

2. Buy a burger for a homeless person this week.

3. Don't talk so much today. Spend the day listening.

4. Before you go to bed tonight, write a simple note of apology to someone you may have offended.

p. 144

July 7

MORE BABY STEPS

1. Write a thank-you note to someone you've been wanting to thank for a long time.

2. Pinpoint when and where it is most difficult for you to refrain from gossip. Is it with a certain friend, in the locker room, during lunch? Come up with a plan of action to avoid it.

3. Try to go one whole day saying only positive things about others.

p. 144

July 8

Habit 4 is Think Win-Win. Think Win-Win is an attitude toward life, a mental frame of mind that says I can win, and so can you. It's not me or you, it's both of us. Think Win-Win is the foundation for getting along well with other people. It begins with the belief that we are all equal, that no one is inferior or superior to anyone else, and no one really needs to be.

pp. 146–47

July 9

It's important to know what Think Win-Win is *not*. Think Win-Win is not Win-Lose. Win-Lose is an attitude toward life that says the pie of success is only so big, and if you get a big piece there is less for me. So I'm going to make sure I get my slice first or that I get a bigger piece than you. Win-Lose is competitive. I call it the totem pole syndrome. "I don't care how good I am as long as I'm a notch higher than you on the totem pole." Relationships, friendships, and loyalty are secondary to winning the game, being the best, and having it your way.

pp. 147–48

July 10

In the end, a Win-Lose attitude will usually back-fire. You may end up on the top of the totem pole. But you'll be there alone and without friends.

p. 149

July 11

Win-Win is also very different from Lose-Win, the doormat syndrome. Lose-Win looks prettier on the surface, but it's just as dangerous as Win-Lose. Lose-Win says, "Have your way with me. Wipe your feet on me. Everyone else does." Lose-Win is weak. It's easy to get stepped on. It's easy to be the nice guy. It's easy to give in, all in the name of being a peacemaker. With a Lose-Win attitude you'll find yourself setting low expectations and compromising your standards again and again. Giving in to peer pressure is Lose-Win.

pp. 149–50

July 12

Let others win the little issues, and it will be a deposit into their RBA. Just be sure you take a stand on the important things.

p. 151

July 13

Finally, Win-Win is not Lose-Lose, the downward spiral. Lose-Lose says, "If I'm going down, then you're going down with me, sucker." After all, misery loves company. If you're not careful, boyfriend-girlfriend relationships can sour into Lose-Lose. You've seen it. Two good people begin dating and things go well at first. It's Win-Win. But gradually they become emotionally glued and co-dependent. They begin to get possessive and jealous. Eventually, this dependency brings out the worst in both of them. They begin to fight, argue, and "get back at" each other, resulting in the downward spiral of Lose-Lose.

pp. 151–52

July 14

Win-Win is the all-you-can-eat buffet. Win-Win is a belief that everyone can win. It's both nice and tough all at once. I won't step on you, but I won't be your doormat either. You care about other people and you want them to succeed. But you also care about yourself, and you want to succeed as well. Win-Win is abundant. It's not either you or me. It's both of us. It's not a matter of who gets the biggest piece of pie. There's more than enough food for everyone.

p. 152

July 15

These are examples of the Win-Win attitude:

- You recently got a promotion at the burger joint you work at. You share the praise and recognition with all of those who helped you get there.

- You were just elected to an important school office and you make up your mind not to develop a "superiority complex." You treat everyone the same, including the friendless and the unpopular.

- Your best friend just got accepted at the college you wanted to get into. You didn't make it. Although you feel terrible about your own situation, you are genuinely happy for your friend.

pp. 153–54

July 16

Personal security is the foundation for thinking Win-Win.

p. 154

July 17

There are two habits that, like tumors, can slowly eat you away from the inside. They are twins and their names are competing and comparing.

p. 155

July 18

"If you base your self-esteem, your feeling of self-worth, on anything outside the quality of your heart, your mind, or your soul, you have based it on a very shaky footing."

—PAUL H. DUNN, "ON FEELING INFERIOR"

p. 157

July 19

Comparing yourself to others can become an addiction as strong as drugs or alcohol. You don't have to look like or dress like a model to be good enough. You know what really matters. Don't get caught up in the game and worry so much about being popular during your teen years, because most of life comes after.

p. 158

July 20

Sometimes, no matter how hard you try, you won't be able to find a Win-Win solution. If you can't find a solution that works for both of you, decide not to play. No Deal. If you and a friend can't agree on an activity one night, split up and get together another night. Or, on a more serious note, if you and your girlfriend or boyfriend can't develop a Win-Win relationship, it might be best for you to go No Deal and part ways.

pp. 159–60

July 21

Developing a Win-Win attitude is not easy. But you can do it. If you're thinking Win-Win only 10 percent of the time right now, start thinking it 20 percent of the time, then 30 percent, and so on. Eventually, it will become a mental habit, and you won't even have to think about it. It will become part of who you are.

pp. 160–61

July 22

Think of a person who you feel is a model of Win-Win. What is it about this person you admire?

p. 162

July 23

Do you have an important test soon? If so, form a study group and share your best ideas with each other. You'll all do better.

p. 162

July 24

BABY STEPS

1. Pinpoint the area of your life where you most struggle with comparisons. Perhaps it's with clothes, physical features, friends, or talents.

2. If you play sports, show sportsmanship. Compliment someone from the opposing team after the match or game.

3. If someone owes you money, don't be afraid to mention it in a friendly way. "Did you forget about that ten bucks I loaned you last week? I could use it right now." Think Win-Win, not Lose-Win.

p. 162

July 25

MORE BABY STEPS

1. Without caring whether you win or lose, play a card, board, or computer game with others just for the fun of it.

2. Are you in a Lose-Win relationship with a member of the opposite sex? If you are, then decide what must happen to make it a Win for you too or choose to go for No Deal and get out of the relationship.

p. 162

HABIT 5
SEEK FIRST TO UNDERSTAND,
THEN TO BE UNDERSTOOD

July 26

"Before I can walk in another's shoes,
I must first remove my own."

—UNKNOWN

209

July 27

Habit 5 is Seek First to Understand, Then to Be Understood. This means seeing things from another's point of view before sharing your own—a whole new world of understanding will be opened up to you.

p. 165

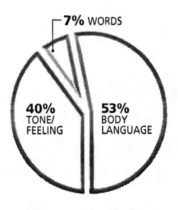

July 28

Habit 5 is the key to communication. The deepest need of the human heart is to be understood. Everyone wants to be respected and valued for who they are—a unique, one-of-a-kind, never-to-be-cloned (at least for now) individual.

p. 165

July 29

People won't expose their soft middles unless they feel genuine love and understanding.

p. 165

July 30

Have you ever heard the saying "People don't care how much you know until they know how much you care?" How true it is. Think about a situation when someone didn't take the time to understand or listen to you. Were you open to what they had to say?

p. 166

July 31

Please Listen

When I ask you to listen to me
and you start giving me advice,
you have not done what I asked.
When I ask you to listen to me
and you begin to tell me why
I shouldn't feel that way,
you are trampling on my feelings.
When I ask you to listen to me
and you feel you have to do something
to solve my problem,
you have failed me,
strange as that may seem.
Listen! All I ask is that you listen.
Don't talk or do—just hear me.

—UNKNOWN

p. 167

August 1

FIVE POOR LISTENING STYLES

- Spacing out
- Pretend listening
- Selective listening
- Word listening
- Self-centered listening

p. 168

August 2

Don't space out when someone is talking to you. They may have something very important to say, and if you're caught up in your own thoughts all the time you'll miss it.

p. 168

August 3

If you only pretend to listen to someone, by saying "yeah," "uh-huh," and "cool" at key junctures in the conversation, the speaker will usually get the hint and will feel that he or she is not important enough to be heard.

p. 168

August 4

If in conversation with other people, you always talk about what you want to talk about, instead of what the other person wants to talk about, chances are you'll never develop lasting friendships.

pp. 168–69

August 5

Word listening occurs when we actually pay attention to what someone is saying, but we listen only to the words, not to the body language, the feelings, or the true meaning behind the words. As a result, we miss out on what's really being said.

p. 169

August 6

Self-centered listening happens when we see everything from our own point of view. Instead of standing in another's shoes, we want them to stand in ours. This is where sentences like "Oh, I know exactly how you feel" come from. We don't know exactly how they feel, we know exactly how we feel, and we assume they feel the same way we do, like the shoe salesman who thinks that you should like the shoes because he likes them.

p. 169

August 7

When we are so busy judging what someone else is saying to us, we don't hear a word that person is saying and we miss out on an opportunity to make a deposit into his or her Relationship Bank Account.

p. 170

August 8

Although we feel the impulse to give advice when someone comes to us with a problem, it is important to remember that sometimes people just want to be understood, not advised. Once someone feels understood, they are more open to our advice.

p. 170

August 9

No one likes to be interrogated. If you're asking someone who has come to you with a problem a lot of questions and you're not getting very far, you're probably probing. Sometimes people just aren't prepared to open up and don't feel like talking. Learn to be a great listener and offer an open ear when the time is right.

p. 170

August 10

In order to be a genuine listener you must first listen with your eyes, heart, and ears.

p. 171

August 11

Sometimes, to hear what other people are really saying, you need to listen to what they are *not* saying.

p. 171

August 12

No matter how hard people may appear on the surface, most everyone is tender inside and has a desperate need to be understood.

p. 171

August 13

"Until you walk a mile in another man's moccasins
you can't imagine the smell."

—ROBERT BYRNE

p. 172

August 14

If you want to improve your relationship with Mom or Dad (and shock the heck out of 'em in the process), try listening to them, just like you would a friend. Now, it may seem kind of weird to treat your parents as if they were normal people and all, but it's worth trying.

pp. 176–77

August 15

If you take the time to understand and listen to your parents, two incredible things will happen. First, you'll gain a greater respect for them. Second, you'll get your way much more often. This isn't a manipulative trick, it's a principle. If they feel that you understand them, they'll be much more willing to listen to you, they'll be more flexible, and they'll trust you more.

p. 177

August 16

Ask yourself, "What do my parents consider a deposit into their Relationship Bank Account?" Jump into their shoes and think about it from their point of view, not yours. A deposit to them might mean doing the dishes or taking out the garbage without being asked, or keeping a commitment to be home on time, or, if you're living away from home, calling them every weekend.

p. 178

August 17

Seeking first to understand requires consideration, but seeking to be understood requires courage.

p. 178

August 18

Unexpressed feelings never die. They are buried alive and come forth later in uglier ways. You've got to share your feelings or they'll eat your heart out. If you have taken time to listen, your chances of being listened to are very good.

p. 178

August 19

Giving feedback is an important part of seeking to be understood. If done in the right way it can be a deposit in the RBA. If someone's fly is open, for instance, give feedback. They'll be grateful, believe me. If you have a close friend who has bad breath (to the point of developing a reputation for it), don't you think he or she would appreciate some honest feedback, delivered tenderly? Have you ever returned home from a date only to discover that you had a big piece of meat between your teeth the whole evening? With terror you immediately recall every smile you made that night. Don't you wish your date had told you?

pp. 178–79

August 20

If your RBA with someone is high, you can give feedback openly without hesitation.

p. 179

August 21

If your motive for giving someone feedback isn't in the other person's best interest, then it's probably not the time or place to do it.

p. 179

August 22

When giving feedback, send "I" messages instead of "you" messages. In other words, give feedback in the first person. Say, "*I'm* concerned that you have a temper problem" or "*I* feel that you've been acting selfish lately." "You" messages are more threatening because they sound as if you're labeling. "*You* are so self-centered." "*You* have a terrible temper."

p. 179

August 23

You have two ears and one mouth—use them accordingly.

p. 179

August 24

See how long you can keep eye contact with someone while they are talking to you.

p. 180

August 25

Go to the mall, find a seat, and watch people communicate with each other. Observe what their body language is saying.

p. 180

August 26

BABY STEPS

1. Sometime this week, ask your mom or dad, "How's it going?" Open up your heart and practice genuine listening. You'll be surprised by what you learn.

2. If you're a talker, take a break and spend your day listening. Only talk when you have to.

3. The next time you find yourself wanting to bury your feelings deep inside you, don't do it. Instead, express them in a responsible way.

p. 180

August 27

Habit 6 is Synergize. What does *Synergize* mean? In a nutshell, synergy is achieved when two or more people work together to create a better solution than either person could alone. It's not your way or my way but a better way, a higher way.

p. 182

Synergy doesn't
just happen.
It's a process.
You have to get
there.

August 28

"Alone we can do so little;
together we can do so much."

—HELEN KELLER

p. 182

August 29

Synergy is everywhere in nature. The great sequoia trees (which grow to heights of 300 feet or more) grow in clumps and share a vast array of intermingled roots. Without each other they would blow over in a storm.

p. 183

August 30

Synergy isn't anything new. If you've ever been on a team of any kind, you've felt it. If you've ever worked on a group project that really came together or been on a really fun group date, you've felt it. Think of all of the instances of synergy in your daily life.

p. 183

August 31

A good band is a great example of synergy. It's not just the drums, or the guitar, or the sax, or the vocalist, it's all of them together that make up the "sound." Each band member brings his or her strengths to the table to create something better than each could alone. No instrument is more important than another, just different.

p. 183

September 1

SYNERGY IS:	SYNERGY IS NOT:
Celebrating differences	Tolerating differences
Teamwork	Working independently
Open-mindedness	Thinking you're always right
Finding new and better ways	Compromise

p. 183

September 2

Synergy doesn't just happen. It's a process. You have to get there. And the foundation of getting there is this: Learn to celebrate differences.

p. 183

September 3

When we hear the word *diversity* we typically think of racial and gender differences. But there is so much more to it, including differences in physical features, dress, language, wealth, family, religious beliefs, lifestyle, education, interests, skills, age, style, and on and on.

p. 184

September 4

People who celebrate diversity value differences. They see them as an advantage, not a weakness. They've learned that two people who think differently can achieve more than two people who think alike. They realize that celebrating differences doesn't mean that you necessarily agree with those differences, such as being a Democrat or a Republican, only that you value them.

p. 185

September 5

Diversity = Creative Sparks = Opportunity

p. 185

September 6

It's much easier to appreciate differences when we realize that in one way or another, we are all a minority of one. And we should remember that diversity isn't just an external thing, it's also internal. In the book *All I Really Need to Know I Learned in Kindergarten*, Robert Fulghum says, "We are as different from one another on the inside of our heads as we appear to be different from one another on the outside of our heads."

p. 186

September 7

Instead of trying to blend in and be like everyone else, be proud of and celebrate your unique differences and qualities. A fruit salad is delicious precisely because each fruit maintains its own flavor.

p. 190

September 8

Although there are many, three of the largest roadblocks to synergy are ignorance, cliques, and prejudice.

p. 190

September 9

There's nothing wrong with wanting to be with those you're comfortable with; it becomes a problem only when your group of friends becomes so exclusive that they begin to reject everyone who isn't just like them. It's kind of hard to value differences in a close-knit clique. Those on the outside feel like second-class citizens, and those on the inside often suffer from superiority complexes. But breaking into a clique isn't hard. All you have to do is lose your identity, be assimilated, and become part of the Borg collective.

p. 191

September 10

Have you ever felt stereotyped, labeled, or prejudged by someone because your skin's the wrong color, your accent's too heavy, or you live on the wrong side of the tracks? Haven't we all, and isn't it a sick feeling?

p. 191

September 11

We aren't born with prejudices. They're learned. Kids, for instance, are color-blind. But as they mature they begin to pick up on the prejudices of others and form walls.

pp. 191–92

September 12

The Cold Within

Six humans trapped by happenstance, in bleak and bitter cold,
Each one possessed a stick of wood, or so the story's told,
Their dying fire in need of logs, the first man held his back,
For of the faces 'round the fire, he noticed one was black.
The next man looking 'cross the way saw one not of his church,
And couldn't bring himself to give the fire his stick of birch.
The third one sat in tattered clothes, he gave his coat a hitch,
Why should his log be put to use to warm the idle rich.
The rich man just sat back and thought of the wealth
he had in store,
And how to keep what he had earned from the lazy, shiftless poor.
The black man's face bespoke revenge as the fire
passed from sight.
For all he saw in his stick of wood was a chance to spite the white.
The last man of this forlorn group did naught except for gain,
Giving only to those who gave was how he played the game.
Their logs held tight in death's still hand was proof of human sin,
They didn't die from the cold without—they died
from the cold within.

—UNKNOWN

p. 192

September 13

Synergy is more than just compromise or cooperation. Compromise is $1 + 1 = 1½$. Cooperation is $1 + 1 = 2$. Synergy is $1 + 1 = 3$ or more. It's creative cooperation, with an emphasis on the word *creative*. The whole is greater than the sum of the parts.

p. 193

September 14

Whether you're arguing with your parents over dating and curfew guidelines or planning a school activity with your peers, or simply not seeing eye to eye, there is a way to *get to synergy*. Here's a simple five-step process to help you get there:

THE GETTING TO SYNERGY ACTION PLAN

1. Define the problem or opportunity.

2. Their way (seek first to understand the ideas of others).

3. My way (seek to be understood by sharing your ideas).

4. Brainstorm (create new options and ideas).

5. High way (find the best solution).

p. 195

September 15

The Getting to Synergy Action Plan can be used in all kinds of situations:

- You've just been assigned a group project for biology with three people you don't even know.

- You and your boyfriend can't decide whose family you should spend Thanksgiving with.

- You want to go to college, but your parents aren't willing to help you pay for it.

- As a student body officer, you and your team are in charge of planning the biggest dance of the year.

- You and your stepmom disagree on your curfew.

- You're always fighting with your brother over the computer.

p. 198

September 16

Great teamwork is like a great piece of music. All the voices and instruments may be singing and playing at once, but they aren't competing. Individually, the instruments and voices make different sounds, play different notes, pause at different times; yet they blend together to create a whole new sound. This is synergy.

p. 200

September 17

"Even when you've played the game of your life, it's the feeling of teamwork that you'll remember. You'll forget the plays, the shots, and the scores, but you'll never forget your teammates."

—DEBORAH MILLER PALMORE,
BASKETBALL OLYMPIAN

p. 201

September 18

When you meet a classmate or neighbor with a disability or impairment, don't feel sorry for them or avoid them because you don't know what to say. Instead, go out of your way to get acquainted.

p. 202

September 19

Share a personal problem with an adult you trust. See if the exchanging of viewpoints leads to new insights and ideas about your problem.

p. 202

September 20

Brainstorm with your friends and come up with something fun, new, and different to do this weekend, instead of doing the same old thing again and again.

p. 202

September 21

1. Think about someone who irritates you. What is different about them? What can you learn from them?

2. Rate your openness to diversity in each of the following categories. Ask yourself: "Am I a shunner, tolerator, or celebrator?"

    Race

    Gender

    Religion

    Age

    Dress

p. 202

September 22

Habit 7 is Sharpen the Saw. It's all about keeping your personal self sharp so that you can better deal with life. It means regularly renewing and strengthening the four key dimensions of your life—your body, your mind, your heart, and your soul.

p. 206

September 23

"The time to repair the roof is when the sun
is shining."

—PRESIDENT JOHN F. KENNEDY

p. 206

September 24

The four key dimensions of your life are:

Body—The physical dimension (exercise, eat healthy, sleep well, relax)

Mind—The mental dimension (read, educate, write, learn new skills)

Heart—The emotional dimension (build relationships—relationship bank account, personal bank account—give service, laugh)

Soul—The spiritual dimension (meditate, keep a journal, pray, take in quality media)

p. 206

September 25

The ancient Greeks' famous saying "Nothing over-much" reminds us of the importance of balance and of keeping in touch with all four dimensions of life. Some people spend countless hours building the perfect body but neglect their minds. Others have minds that can bench-press 400 pounds but let their bodies waste away or forget about having a social life. To perform at your peak, you need to strive for balance in all four areas.

p. 207

September 26

Why is balance so important? It's because how you do in one dimension of life will affect the other three. Think about it. If one of your car's tires is out of balance, all four tires will wear unevenly, not just the one. It's hard to be friendly (heart) when you're exhausted (body). It also works the other way. When you're feeling motivated and in tune with yourself (soul), it's easier to focus on your studies (mind) and to be more friendly (heart).

p. 207

September 27

Just like a car, you too need regular tune-ups and oil changes. You need time out to rejuvenate the best thing you've got going for yourself—you! You need time to relax and unstring your bow, time to treat yourself to a little tender loving care. This is what sharpening the saw is all about.

p. 207

September 28

This ever-changing body of yours is really quite a marvelous machine. You can handle it with care or you can abuse it. You can control it or let it control you. In short, your body is a tool, and if you take good care of it, it will serve you well.

p. 208

September 29

Here is a list of ten ways teens can keep their physical selves sharp:

1. Eat good food
2. Relax in the bathtub
3. Bike
4. Lift weights
5. Get enough sleep
6. Practice yoga
7. Play sports
8. Take walks
9. Stretch out
10. Do an aerobics workout

p. 208

September 30

The four key ingredients to a healthy body are good sleeping habits, physical relaxation, good nutrition, and proper exercise.

p. 208

October 1

You are what you eat. Listen to your body. Pay careful attention to how different foods make you feel and from that develop your *own* handful of do's and don'ts.

p. 208

October 2

When it comes to eating, be moderate and avoid extremes. For many of us, it's easier to be extreme than moderate, and so we find ourselves jumping back and forth between eating a rabbit-food diet and a junk-food diet. But extreme eating habits can be unhealthy. A little junk food on occasion isn't going to hurt you. (I mean, what would life be like without an occasional Slurpee?) Just don't make it your everyday fare.

p. 209

October 3

Remember, food affects mood. So eat with care.

p. 209

October 4

We all feel depressed, confused, or apathetic at times. And it's at times like these when perhaps the best thing we can do for ourselves is to do what Forrest Gump did: Exercise ourselves better. Besides being good for your heart and lungs, exercise has an amazing way of giving you a shot of energy, melting stress away, and clearing your mind.

p. 210

October 5

There is no single best way to exercise. Many teenagers like to play competitive sports. Others prefer running, walking, biking, in-line skating, dancing, stretching, aerobics, or lifting weights. Still others like to get outside and move around. For best results, you should exercise for twenty or thirty minutes a session at least three times a week.

p. 210

October 6

Don't let *pain* be the first thing that comes into your mind when you hear the word *exercise*. Instead, find something you enjoy doing, so that it's easy to maintain.

p. 210

October 7

It's all about how you feel, not how you look. In your quest for a better physique, make sure you don't get too obsessed with your appearance. As you've probably noticed, our society is hung up on "looks." To prove my point, just walk into any grocery store and glance at the "perfect" people who adorn the covers of nearly every magazine. (If you don't already know it, what you see on the covers of magazines isn't real. They're "images" touched up and manipulated by a whole team of stylists and designers.)

pp. 210–11

October 8

Before you start comparing yourself to the babes and hunks on the covers of *Cosmopolitan* and *Muscle & Fitness* and begin hating everything about your body and looks, please remember that there are thousands of healthy and happy teens who don't have high cheekbones, rock-hard abs, or buns of steel. There are many successful singers, talk show hosts, dancers, athletes, actors, and actresses who have all kinds of physical imperfections. If you don't have the "look" or body type our society has stamped "ideal," so what? What's popular today will probably change tomorrow anyhow.

p. 211

October 9

The important thing is not your appearance, but feeling good physically. Talk show host Oprah Winfrey said it best: "You have to change your perception. It's not about weight—it's caring for yourself on a daily basis."

p. 211

October 10

We should work hard to look our best and be presentable, but if we aren't careful, becoming obsessed with looks can lead us to eating disorders or addictions to performance-enhancing drugs. Treating your body like a prisoner of war in order to be accepted by someone else is never worth it.

p. 212

October 11

Just as there are ways to care for your body, there are also ways to destroy it. And using addictive substances such as alcohol, drugs, and tobacco is a great way to do it. Alcohol, for example, is often associated with the three leading causes of death among teens: car accidents, suicide, and homicide. And then there's smoking, which has been proven to cloud your eyes, cause your skin to prematurely age, yellow your teeth, cause bad breath, triple your cavities, cause receding gums, discolor the skin on your fingertips, create tiredness, and cause cancer.

p. 212

October 12

Tobacco companies spend $500,000 every hour of every day promoting and advertising cigarettes. They want your money. A pack of cigarettes a day adds up to $1,000 a year. Just think about how many CDs you could buy for $1,000. Don't let them sucker you!

p. 213

October 13

No one plans on getting addicted to drugs. It all starts so innocently. Yet too often playing with "gateway" drugs like alcohol and tobacco leads to marijuana and then on to the other deadly drugs like cocaine, LSD, PCP, opiates, and heroin. Many teens begin drinking, smoking, or doing drugs in an attempt to display their *freedom*, only to find that they eventually develop an addiction that *destroys* their freedom.

p. 213

October 14

Perhaps the worst thing about picking up an addiction is this: You're no longer in control—your addiction is. When it says *jump*, you jump. You react. Say good-bye to the whole idea of being proactive.

p. 213

October 15

We always think addiction is something that happens to someone else and that we could quit anytime. Right? In reality, it's hard. As an example, only 25 percent of teen tobacco users who try to quit are successful. I like what Mark Twain said about how easy it was for him to quit smoking: "I've done it a hundred times."

p. 213

October 16

You're not missing out on anything if you stay away from drugs. "Life itself," said TV chef Julia Child, "is the proper binge."

p. 215

October 17

With drugs, the short-term bang is never worth the long-term devastation that often follows. If you don't smoke, drink, or do drugs, why even start? If you do, why not get help and quit? There are much better and more natural ways to get high. Why not give them a try?

p. 215

October 18

Nothing in life comes easy. You have to pay the price! Everyone has to pay the price. Write that down. Memorize it. Underline it. I don't care what people say, there are no free lunches. In order to secure a good job and a promising future we must pay the price and *develop a strong mind*.

pp. 216–17

October 19

Getting a good education may be the most important price you can pay—because, perhaps more than anything else, what you do with that mass of gray material between your ears will determine your future. In fact, unless you want to be flipping burgers and living with your parents when you're thirty years old, you'd better start paying the price now.

p. 217

October 20

The mental dimension of Habit 7 is every bit as important as the physical dimension. The two support and enhance each other. Develop your brain power through your schooling, extracurricular activities, hobbies, jobs, and other mind-enlarging experiences.

p. 217

October 21

I asked a group of teenagers in a survey, "What are your fears?" I was surprised by how many spoke about the stress of doing well in school, going to college, and getting a good job in the future. Said one, "What can we do to be certain that we can get a job and support ourselves?" The answer is really rather simple: Develop an educated mind. By far, this offers your best chance of securing a good job and making a life for yourself.

p. 217

October 22

An educated mind is like a well-conditioned ballerina. A ballerina has perfect control over her muscles. Her body will bend, twist, jump, and turn perfectly, according to her command. Similarly, an educated mind can focus, synthesize, write, speak, create, analyze, explore, imagine, and so much more. To do that, however, it must be trained. It won't just happen.

p. 217

October 23

Get as much education as you can. Any further education beyond high school—a college degree, vocational or technical training, an apprenticeship, or training in any of the armed forces—will be well worth your time and money. See it as an investment in your future. Statistics have shown that a college graduate earns about twice as much as a high school graduate. And the gap seems to be widening.

pp. 217–18

October 24

"If you think education is expensive,
try ignorance."

—DEREK BOK, FORMER PRESIDENT
OF HARVARD UNIVERSITY

p. 218

October 25

Even if you have to sacrifice and work your tail off to pay for your education, it's well worth it. You'd also be amazed at the number of scholarships, grants, loans, and student-aid options that are available if you search them out. In fact, millions of dollars of grant and scholarship money goes unclaimed each year because no one bothered to apply for it.

p. 218

October 26

There are numerous ways to expand your mind. However, the best approach may simply be to *read*. As the saying goes, reading is to the mind what exercise is to the body. Reading is foundational to everything else and doesn't cost that much, unlike other methods, such as traveling.

p. 218

October 27

Ten possible ways to sharpen your mind:

- Read a newspaper every day
- Subscribe to *National Geographic*
- Travel
- Plant a garden
- Observe wildlife
- Attend a lecture on an interesting topic
- Watch the Discovery Channel
- Visit a library
- Listen to the news
- Research your ancestors

p. 218

October 28

Ten more possible ways to sharpen your mind:

- Write a story, poem, or song
- Play challenging board games
- Debate
- Play a game of chess
- Visit a museum
- Comment in class
- Attend a ballet, opera, or play
- Learn to play a musical instrument
- Have stimulating conversations with friends
- Solve crossword puzzles

p. 218

October 29

Find your niche. While you may need to endure some subjects you don't enjoy at school, find the subjects you do enjoy and build upon them. Take additional classes, check out books, and see movies about the topic. Don't let school be your only form of education. Let the world be your campus.

p. 218

October 30

You should expect to have some trouble in some classes. Unless you're an Einstein, not every subject will be easy for you. Actually I take back what I just said. The famous Albert Einstein actually failed math and was thought a fool for years.

p. 219

October 31

If you ever get discouraged by school, please don't drop out. (You'll live to regret it.) Just keep plugging away. You're bound to eventually find something you enjoy about it or something you can excel at.

p. 219

November 1

Don't let school get in the way of your education. Although grades are important, becoming truly educated is more important, so make sure you don't forget why you're going to school.

pp. 219–20

November 2

Over the years, I've seen so many people sacrifice their education for so many stupid reasons, often on the altar of sports. "A youngster gambling his future on a pro contract is like a worker buying a single Irish Sweepstakes ticket and then quitting his job in anticipation of his winnings," said Senator Bill Bradley, a former NBA star. Studies have shown that only one out of every 100 high school athletes will play Division I college sports, and that the chances of a high school player making the pros are one in ten thousand.

pp. 220–21

November 3

You say you don't like school. I say, What does that have to do with it? Does anything good in life come easy? Does an athlete like working out every day? Does a medical student enjoy studying non-stop for four years? Since when does liking something determine whether or not you should do it? Sometimes you just have to discipline yourself to do things you don't feel like doing because of what you hope to gain from it.

p. 222

November 4

You say that you try to study but can't because your mind begins to wander. I say that unless you learn to control your mind you won't amount to squat. The discipline of the mind is a much higher form of discipline than that of the body.

p. 222

November 5

You say you can get by without studying, that by cramming and finding ways to beat the system you can pull out passing grades. I say you reap what you sow. Can the farmer cram? Can he forget to plant his crops in the spring, loaf all summer long, and then work real hard to bring in the harvest? Can you improve your bench press by lifting weights once in a while? Your brain is no different than your biceps. Don't expect to show up one day in the Land of Oz and have the Wizard hand you a brain.

p. 222

November 6

Imagine five sets of hands. One set belongs to a concert pianist who can enthrall audiences. Another to an eye surgeon who can restore lost vision. Another to a professional golfer who consistently makes the shot under pressure. Another to a blind man who can read tiny raised markings on a page at incredible speed. Another to an artist who can carve beautiful sculptures that inspire the soul. On the surface, the hands may all look the same, but behind each set are years and years of sacrifice, discipline, and perseverance. These people paid a price! They did not cram. They did not beat the system.

p. 222

November 7

If you don't pay the price you will earn a degree but fail to get an education. There is a big difference between the two.

p. 223

November 8

Some of our best thinkers were degreeless, self-educated men and women. How did they do it? They read. It's only the single greatest habit you could ever develop. Many people stop reading and learning when they finish school. That spells brain atrophy. Education must be a lifelong pursuit.

p. 223

November 9

The person who doesn't read is no better off than the person who can't.

p. 223

November 10

Don't make long-term career decisions based on short-term emotions, like the student who chooses his or her major based on the shortest registration line. Develop a future orientation; make decisions with the end in mind.

p. 223

November 11

The Proverb sums up the whole matter: "Take fast hold of instruction; let her not go: keep her, for she is thy life."

p. 223

November 12

Don't get too worried about your major or area of focus in school. If you can simply learn to think well, you will have plenty of career and education options to choose from. Admissions offices and companies that are hiring don't care so much about what you majored in. They want to see evidence that you have a sound mind.

p. 224

November 13

Admissions offices and companies will be looking at several different areas:

1. Desire—How badly do you want to get into this particular school or program? How much do you want this job?

2. Standardized test scores—How well did you score on your ACT, SAT, GRE, LSAT, etc.?

3. Extracurricular—What other activities were you involved in?

4. Letters of recommendation—What do other people think of you?

5. Grade point average—How well did you do in school?

6. Communication skills—How well can you communicate in writing (based on your application essays) and verbally (based on an interview)?

p. 224

November 14

Don't be scared off by rumors about how hard it is to get into college or other schools. It's usually not as hard as you might think if you're willing to put some effort into your application.

p. 224

November 15

As you attempt to build a brain, you will need to overcome a few barriers. One is *screentime,* any time spent in front of a screen, like a TV, computer, video game, or movie screen. *Some* time can be healthy, but *too much* time can numb your mind.

p. 226

November 16

Interestingly, some teens don't want to do too well in school because others might think they're too studious (nerds), and studious isn't cool. If having a mind intimidates someone, that probably tells you something about their own lack of neurons. Take pride in your mental abilities and the fact that you value education. There are a lot of wealthy and successful people who were once considered nerds.

p. 226

November 17

Sometimes we're scared of doing well in school because of the high expectations it creates. Just remember this: The stress that results from success is much more tolerable than the regret that results from not trying your best. Don't sweat the pressure. You can deal with it.

p. 226

November 18

You gotta wanna. In the end, the key to honing your mind will be your desire to learn. You've gotta really want it. You've gotta get turned on by learning. You've gotta pay the price.

p. 226

November 19

If you haven't paid the price to educate yourself so far, it's never too late to start. If you can learn to think well, the future will be an open door of opportunity. It's all about brain waves. Get some.

p. 227

November 20

Do you ever feel that you're the moodiest person in the world and that you can't control your emotions? If you do, then welcome to the club, because those feelings are pretty normal for teens. You see, your heart is a very temperamental thing. And it needs constant nourishment and care, just like your body.

p. 228

November 21

The best way to sharpen the saw and nourish your heart is to focus on building relationships, or in other words, to make regular deposits into your relationship bank accounts and into your own personal bank account.

p. 228

November 22

"Let no one ever come to you without leaving better and happier. Be the living expression of God's kindness: kindness in your face, kindness in your eyes, kindness in your smile."

—MOTHER TERESA

p. 228

November 23

Remember, PBA and RBA deposits are very similar. That's because deposits you make into other people's accounts usually end up in your own as well.

p. 229

November 24

As you set out each day, look for opportunities to make deposits and build lasting friendships. Listen deeply to a friend, parent, brother, or sister without expecting anything in return. Give out ten compliments today. Stick up for someone. Come home when you told your parents you'd be home.

p. 229

November 25

Sex is about a whole lot more than your body. It's also about your heart. In fact, what you do about sex may affect your self-image and your relationships with others more than any other decision you make. Before you decide to have sex or to continue having it, search your heart and think about it . . . carefully.

pp. 229–30

November 26

It's totally normal to feel depressed at times. But there is a big difference between a case of the blues and sustained depression. If life has become a real pain for a long period of time and you can't seem to shake off that feeling of hopelessness, things are serious. Fortunately, depression is treatable. Don't hesitate to get help, either from medication or from talking with someone who is trained to deal with these issues.

pp. 231–32

November 27

Remember that the struggles you are now facing will eventually become a great source of strength for you. As the philosopher Kahlil Gibran wrote: "That self-same well from which our laughter rises was often times filled with our tears. The deeper that sorrow carries into our being, the more joy it can contain."

p. 232

November 28

After all is said and done, there is one last key to keeping your heart healthy and strong. Just laugh. That's right . . . laugh. *Hakuna matata!* Don't worry, be happy! Sometimes life just sucks and there's not much you can do to change it, so you might as well laugh.

p. 232

November 29

It's too bad that as we age we tend to forget what made childhood so magical. One study showed that by the time you reach kindergarten, you laugh about 300 times a day. In contrast, the typical adult laughs a wimpy seventeen times a day. Why are we so serious? Maybe it's because we've been taught that laughing too much is childish. We must learn to laugh again.

pp. 232–33

November 30

I read the most fascinating article in *Psychology Today* by Peter Doskoch about the power of humor. Here were some of his key findings:
Laughter:

- Loosens up the mental gears and helps us think more creatively.

- Helps us cope with the difficulties of life.

- Reduces stress levels.

- Relaxes us as it lowers our heart rate and blood pressure.

- Connects us with others and counteracts feelings of alienation.

- Releases endorphins, the brain's natural painkillers.

p. 233

December 1

Laughter has also been shown to promote good health and speed healing. I've heard several accounts of people who healed themselves from serious sickness through heavy doses of laughing therapy.

p. 233

December 2

Laughter can also help heal injured relationships. As entertainer Victor Borge put it, "Laughter is the shortest distance between two people."

p. 233

December 3

If you're not laughing much, what can you do to start again? I suggest developing your own "humor collection," a collection of books, cartoons, videos, ideas—whatever is funny to you. Then, whenever you're feeling down, or taking yourself way too seriously, visit your collection.

p. 233

December 4

Learn to laugh at yourself when strange or funny things happen to you, because they will. As someone once said, "One of the best things people can have up their sleeve is a good funny bone."

p. 233

December 5

What is it that moves your soul? A great movie? A good book? Have you ever seen a movie that made you cry? What was it that got to you? Think about it.

p. 234

December 6

What deeply inspires you? Find time to be close to, watch, listen to, read about those things and people that inspire you in different ways.

p. 234

December 7

Your soul is your center, wherein lie your deepest convictions and values. It is the source for purpose, meaning, and inner peace. Sharpening the saw in the spiritual area of life means taking time to renew and awaken that inner self.

p. 234

December 8

"Inside myself is a place where I live all alone and that's where you renew your springs that never dry up."

—PEARL S. BUCK

p. 234

December 9

Your soul is a very private area of your life. Naturally, there are many different ways to feed it. Here are a few ideas shared by teens:

- Meditating
- Serving others
- Writing in a journal
- Going for a walk
- Reading inspiring books
- Drawing
- Praying
- Writing poetry or music

p. 234

December 10

More ways to feed the soul:

- Thinking deeply
- Listening to uplifting music
- Playing a musical instrument
- Practicing a religion
- Talking to friends I can be myself with
- Reflecting on my goals or mission statement

pp. 234–35

December 11

There is something magical about getting into nature that just can't be matched. Even if you live in a downtown area far removed from rivers, mountains, or beaches, there will usually be a park nearby that you can visit.

p. 235

December 12

Keeping a journal can do wonders for your soul. It can become your solace, your best friend, the only place where you can fully express yourself no matter how angry, happy, scared, love-crazed, insecure, or confused you feel. You can pour your heart out in your journal and it will just sit there and listen.

p. 235

December 13

There is no formal way to keep a journal. Feel free to paste in mementos, ticket stubs, love notes, and anything else that will preserve a memory. My old journals are full of poor art, bad poetry, and strange smells.

p. 236

December 14

Keeping a journal will strengthen your tool of self-awareness. It's fun and enlightening to read past entries and realize how much you've grown, how stupid and immature you were with some boy or girl. Reading back through a journal gives insight into our behavior and development.

p. 236

December 15

A journal is just a formal name for putting your thoughts down on paper. There are other names and forms. Some people write notes to themselves, others keep a "gratitude book."

p. 236

December 16

I've often wondered what would happen to someone who drank and ate only soft drinks and chocolate for several years straight. What would they look and feel like after a while? Probably like scum. But why do we think the result would be any different if we fed our soul trash for several years straight? You're not only what you eat, you're also what you listen to, read, and see. More important than what goes into your body is what goes into your soul.

pp. 236–37

December 17

What is your spiritual diet? Are you feeding your soul nutrients, or are you loading it with nuclear waste? What kind of media do you allow yourself to take in? Have you ever even thought about it?

p. 237

December 18

If you think the media doesn't affect you, just think about your favorite song and what it does to your emotions. Or think about the last time you saw half-naked members of the opposite sex wiggling all over the screen or pictured on the page. Or think back to the last bottle of shampoo you bought. Why did you buy it? Probably because of the influence of a thirty-second TV commercial or a one-page magazine ad. And if a one-page ad can sell a bottle of shampoo, don't you think a full-length movie, magazine, or CD can sell a lifestyle?

p. 237

December 19

Addictions of all kinds—whether it's to drugs, gossiping, shopping, overeating, or gambling—have common characteristics. Addiction:

- Creates short-term pleasure.

- Becomes the primary focus of your life.

- Temporarily eliminates pain.

- Gives an artificial sense of self-worth, power, control, security, and intimacy.

- Worsens the problems and feelings you are trying to escape from.

pp. 238–39

December 20

There is a time for everything. A time to be balanced and a time to be imbalanced. There are times when you'll need to go without much sleep and push your body to its limit, for a day, a week, or a season. And there will be times when eating junk food out of the vending machine is your only alternative to starving. This is real life. But there are also times for renewal.

p. 240

December 21

You're probably already doing a lot of saw sharpening without even knowing it. If you're working hard at school, you're sharpening your mind. If you're into athletics or fitness, you're caring for your body. If you're working to develop friendships, you're nourishing your heart. Often you can sharpen the saw in more than one area at once.

p. 241

December 22

The best thing to do is to take out time each day to sharpen the saw, even if it's only for fifteen or thirty minutes. Some teens set apart a specific time each day—early in the morning, after school, or late at night—to be alone, to think, or to exercise. Others like to do it on the weekends. There's no one right way—so find what works for you.

p. 241

December 23

Abraham Lincoln was once asked, "What would you do if you had eight hours to cut down a tree?" He replied, "I'd spend the first four hours sharpening my saw."

p. 241

December 24

BABY STEPS

1. Eat breakfast.

2. Give up a bad habit for a week. See how you feel.

3. Go on a one-on-one outing with a family member like your mom or your brother. Catch a ball game, see a movie, go shopping, or get an ice cream.

4. Watch the sunset tonight or get up early to watch the sunrise.

p. 242

December 25

MORE BABY STEPS

1. Subscribe to a magazine that has some educational value, such as *Popular Mechanics* or *National Geographic*.

2. Begin today to build your humor collection. Cut out your favorite cartoons, buy hilarious movies, or start your own collection of great jokes. In no time, you'll have something to go to when you're feeling stressed.

3. If you haven't already done it, start keeping a journal today.

4. Take time each day to meditate, reflect upon your life, or pray. Do what works for you.

p. 242

December 26

If, after reading this book, you feel overwhelmed and don't have a clue where to start, I'd suggest doing this: Thumb through this book quickly for the key ideas, or ask yourself, "Which habit am I having the most difficult time living?" Then choose just two or three things to work on (don't get overzealous and choose twenty). Write them down and put them in a place where you can review them often. Then let them inspire you each day, not send you on a guilt trip.

pp. 243–44

If you'd like to submit your story about applying the 7 Habits in your life for possible future publications, please e-mail it to us at 7Hteen@7Habits.com

December 27

You'll be amazed at the results a few small changes can bring. Gradually, you'll increase in confidence, you'll feel happier, you'll get high "naturally," your goals will become realities, your relationships will improve, and you'll feel at peace. It all begins with a single step.

p. 244

December 28

If you ever find yourself sliding or falling short, *don't get discouraged*. Remember the flight of an airplane. When an airplane takes off it has a flight plan. However, during the course of the flight, wind, rain, turbulence, air traffic, human error, and other factors keep knocking the plane off course. In fact, a plane is off course about 90 percent of the time. The key is that the pilots keep making small course corrections by reading their instruments and talking to the control tower. If you just keep coming back to your plan, keep making small adjustments, and keep hope alive, you eventually reach your destination.

p. 244

December 29

I wrote this book to give you hope. Hope that you can change, kick an addiction, improve an important relationship. Hope that you can find answers to your problems and reach your fullest potential. So what if your family life stinks, you're failing school, and the only good relationship you have is with your cat (and lately she's been letting you down). *Keep hope alive!*

p. 243

December 30

You are destined for great things. Always remember, you were born with everything you need to succeed. You don't have to look anywhere else. The power and light are in you!

p. 244

December 31

"You can't make footprints in the sands of time by sitting on your butt. And who wants to leave buttprints in the sands of time?"

—BOB MOAWAD

p. 244

What Teens and Others Are Saying About
The 7 Habits of Highly Effective Teens

"Sean Covey's *The 7 Habits of Highly Effective Teens* is a true gift for the 'teenage soul.' No matter what issues you may be struggling with in life, this book offers hope, vision, and the strength to overcome your challenges."

—Jack Canfield and Kimberly Kirberger,
co-authors of *Chicken Soup for the Teenage Soul*

"This is an easy-to-understand book full of interesting stories. I really related to Sean's personal story about the fear of performing in front of people since I am a violinist. I'm sure teenagers around the globe will be able to relate as well."

—Emily Inouye, age 14

"Sean Covey speaks to teenagers in a way that is both entertaining and thought-provoking. His message offers teens a solid road map to a successful future. I highly recommend it."

—John Gray, author of *Men Are from Mars, Women Are from Venus*

"*The 7 Habits of Highly Effective Teens* is a real-life guide to help teens be their best. Setting goals and writing them down is one of the most important things you can do. Commit them to memory, stay focused, and develop the stamina to go the distance. If you do, you can achieve any goal you set."

—Tara Lipinski, U.S. Figure Skating Champion
and 1998 Olympic Gold Medalist

"The inspiring examples from real-life problems that teenagers like myself deal with every day, and their experiences and situations, have helped me make life-saving decisions. I highly recommend this book to any teenager."

—Jeremy Sommer, age 19

"If *The 7 Habits of Highly Effective Teens* doesn't help you, then you must have a perfect life already."

—Jordan McLaughlin, age 17

About Franklin Covey Co.

Sean Covey is vice president of retail stores at Franklin Covey Co., a 4,500-member international firm devoted to helping individuals, organizations, and families become more effective. Franklin Covey Co. is the leading global provider of integrated, sustainable professional services and product solutions based on proven principles. The company's client portfolio includes eighty-two of the Fortune 100 companies, more than two-thirds of the Fortune 500 companies, as well as thousands of small and midsize companies, and government entities, educational institutions, communities, families, and millions of individual consumers. Franklin Covey Co. has also created pilot partnerships with cities seeking to become principle-centered communities, and is currently teaching the 7 Habits to teachers and administrators in more than 4,500 schools and universities nationwide and through statewide initiatives with education leaders in twenty-seven states.

Franklin Covey Co. has more than 19,000 licensed client facilitators teaching its curriculum within their organizations, and it trains in excess of 750,000 participants annually. Implementation tools, including the Franklin Planner, the 7 Habits Organizer, and a wide offering of audio- and videotapes, books, and computer software programs, enable clients to retain and effectively utilize concepts and skills. These and other products carefully selected and endorsed by Franklin Covey Co. are available in more than 125 Franklin Covey Stores throughout North America and in several other countries. Franklin Covey Co. products and materials are now available in thirty-two languages, and its planner products are used by more than 15 million individuals worldwide. The company has more than 15 million books in print, with more than 1.5 million sold each year.

For more information on the Franklin Covey Store or International Office closest to you, or for a free catalog of Franklin Covey products and programs, call or write:

Franklin Covey Company

2200 West Parkway Boulevard
Salt Lake City, Utah 84119-2331 USA
Toll Free: 800-952-6839
Fax: 801-496-4252
International callers: 801-229-1333
or fax 801-229-1233
Internet: http://www.franklincovey.com

Franklin Covey's products and programs provide a wide range of resources for individuals, families, and business, government, nonprofit, and education organizations, including:

PROGRAMS	PRODUCTS
Leadership Week	Collegiate Planner
The 4 Roles of Leadership	Premier School Agendas
The 7 Habits of Highly Effective People	Franklin Planner
What Matters Most Time Management	PalmPilot with Franklin Planner software
The Power Principle	7 Habits Coach
The Best of Both Worlds—Work-Life Balance	On Target Project Management software
Planning for Results	7 Habits audiotapes
Presentation Advantage	Living the 7 Habits audiotapes
Writing Advantage	Principle-Centered Leadership audiotapes
Building Trust	First Things First audiotapes
Getting to Synergy	

Want to be in our next book?

Then tell us your story! Perhaps you have your own story of using 7 Habits principles to overcome challenges personally, in your family, with your friends, or at work or school. Or perhaps you've heard of one. Write us about those experiences and how you were motivated to succeed. If we accept your story, you'll be in our next 7 Habits for Teens book.

Send your entry to:

e-mail: *7Hteen@7Habits.com*
or log on at: *www.franklincovey.com*

Fax: (801) 496-4225
Attn: 7Hteen

Mail:
Franklin Covey Co.
Attn: MS2233/Teen Dept.
466 West 4800 North
Provo, UT 84606-4478
USA

Be sure to make a copy, as we cannot return submissions!